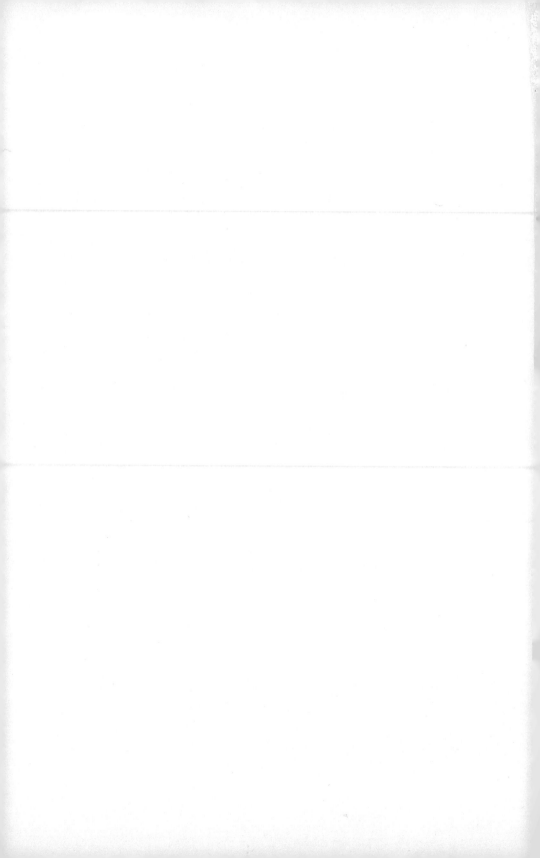

How
Lawyers
Screw
Their
Clients *and*
What You Can
Do About It

How Lawyers Screw Their Clients *and* What You Can Do About It

DONALD E. DEKIEFFER, ESQ.

BARNES
&NOBLE
BOOKS
NEW YORK

Contents

BOOK I

How Law Firms Overcharge
—How To Fight Back

BOOK II

How Law Firms Can Prosper by Joining the Market Economy

Introduction

Everyone complains about health-care costs and, indeed, health care is one of the fastest-growing, major expenses in the American economy; it presents a serious challenge to the very viability of the American economy. Less noticed, but equally insidious, is the rise in legal costs.

Consider the following:

◆ Between 1980 and 1988, the number of lawyers in the country rose from 542,205 to 723,189, a 33 percent increase.

◆ According to the *Statistical Abstract of the United States*, legal fees paid to private practitioners amounted to more than $83 billion in 1989. In 1980 there was one lawyer per 403 people in the United States, by 1990 that number rose to one lawyer per 340, and by the year 2000, the proportion is estimated to be one lawyer per 300 people.

Several Japanese politicians have criticized the United States for devoting more resources to Wall Street than manufacturing.

They might well have been referring to the growth of the legal profession. Many of our best and brightest are entering the law rather than other professions for a simple reason: it can be extremely lucrative.

And what does society get from this? It is incontestable that every free society needs lawyers. Law has grown so complex that specialists are necessary to defend the powerless, negotiate complex contracts, and interpret the tax codes. Lawyers are also essential to assure compliance and enforcement of hundreds of laws that society has deemed desirable, including environmental protection, antidiscrimination, worker's safety and health, and the protection of intellectual property.

While some increase in lawyers would be inevitable due to the natural growth in population and the increasing complexity of federal, state, and local laws, such natural increases do not explain the explosive growth of law as a profession of choice for college graduates. For many of them, the law is a safe, recession-resistant, and profitable undertaking. One would be hard-pressed, however, to demonstrate that our rights and liberties are 23 percent better protected in 1993 than they were in 1983 (which represents the net increase in lawyers over the natural population growth). Much of the balance of the increase in the number of lawyers is not driven by improvements in justice but improvements in the pocketbooks of the legal profession.

Part of the reason we have more lawyers (and perhaps less justice) today than in former decades has less to do with simple greed than the way in which legal services are billed. This also goes to the heart of why the practice of law is so lucrative. It is profitable in large measure because clients have little concept as to how to control legal fees.

This book will provide a few answers to that problem. It is designed to put consumers of legal services—clients—back in control of their own interests, enabling them to get more legal services for the buck.

Equally important, the book considers how law firms can dump the Soviet economic system it has imposed on itself and join the free market. The law can *still* be a profitable undertaking while delivering greater justice with fewer lawyers at lower cost.

BOOK I

How Law Firms
OVERCHARGE
How To Fight Back

CHAPTER 1

Gross Billable Hours

When you receive a statement from a law firm, it will look impressive. There will probably be a cover letter from a senior partner in the firm, followed by a detailed recitation of all work done on your matters, the time spent by each lawyer working on your project, and a description of the work accomplished. There may also be an out-of-pocket expense bill, listing such items as postage, telephone calls, messenger services, and overtime invested in your project during that billing cycle.

Statements submitted by law firms often appear to be more detailed than those you would receive from other vendors of services, such as your doctor, dentist, or auto mechanic. Faced with such a meticulously prepared statement, most clients do not challenge it.

This is a mistake.

Many law firms are driven by a philosophy of "gross billable hours" by which attorneys are compensated in proportion to the *maximum* time they can take to accomplish a client's objective. This usually has little relationship to the value of the legal services to the client or the amount of time it *should* have taken competent counsel to accomplish the result. Compared with statements from your auto mechanic, most legal statements are grotesquely deficient.

When you take your car for servicing, most dealerships' standard rates will be posted or disclosed on the bill. An oil change, for example, might be posted as costing $25, which represents one-half hour of a mechanic's time at $50 an hour. Car dealerships have developed time/motion studies to determine the average time in which a task can be accomplished. If it is accomplished in less time, you pay the average amount. If it takes more time, you still pay the listed amount. The service department will encourage its staff to work as efficiently as possible. Not so with most law firms.

Clients are rarely advised of average amounts of time to finish a project and are almost *never* billed on this basis. Most firms have adopted a gross billable hours system, which means that clients will pay for work done, however long it takes. This encourages lawyers to expand the time they spend on a project to the maximum extent possible.

Unlike an auto dealership, there is no limit as to how much can be charged. Law firms are motivated to be as *inefficient* as possible. The "gross billable hours" standard not only increases the cost of legal services but distorts the way the practice of law is managed.

This book will examine how the "gross billable hours"[1] standard not only increases the cost of legal services, but distorts the way the practice of law is managed.

Although law firms are big business (some major firms gross more than one-half billion dollars a year), they are not run like almost any other business enterprise on the face of the planet, with the possible exception of ex-Soviet tractor factories in which quotas were everything, regardless of the value of the product to the consumer or the efficiency with which the tractors were produced. Even though the gross billable hours system is inherently inefficient, there will be little pressure to change it unless clients demand it.

The crack has begun in this system, and it will expand rapidly. Efficient law firms will displace the current inefficient ones. Several medium-sized law firms have already recognized that the gross billable hours standard not only penalizes clients but is antithetical to a free-market system. This book examines why this is so and what both clients and law firms can do to slay the gross billable hours dragon.

---

[1] Lawyers are fond of footnotes, but they will be avoided in this book. When coining a phrase, however, I instinctively enclose it in quotations. Hereafter, these chicken scratches will be deleted in the interest of readability.

After the thirty-year-old lawyer died, he screamed at Saint Peter, "How can you do this to me? A heart attack at my age! I'm only thirty."

Replied Saint Peter, "Well, when we looked at your total billable hours, we figured you had to be at least ninety-five."

from Jess M. Brallier's
Lawyers and Other Reptiles

CHAPTER 2

Minimum Hours

"The notion that a partner or an associate must produce 2,000 or 2,400 hours of billable legal work yearly virtually assures that some clients will be over-billed."—Seth Rosner, *American Bar Association Journal*, May 1992.

In many large firms today, partners and associates are expected to log anywhere between 1,800 and 2,400 annual hours on their time sheets. What is actually logged on time sheets does not necessarily represent actual time spent on client matters. Minimum standards for billable time create interesting anomalies. For example, it is not unusual for an attorney to have gross billable hours of 2,000 in a given year. How can this be done? Consider the following.

There are approximately 245 workdays in a year (not including vacation). Assuming an attorney takes a two-week vacation

(10 days per year), this reduces workdays to 235. 235 x 8 = 1,880 available hours per year. Therefore, an attorney must work *more* than 8 hours a day to achieve his 2,000 hour a year goal, take less vacation time, work weekends, or combinations of the above.

Now consider the distinction between billable hours and actual hours. "Billable" hours theoretically represent time actually spent on client matters, not counting such administrative matters as work on firm committees, attendance at professional meetings, routine paperwork, and compiling time sheets. It also does not count getting a cup of coffee, going to the rest room, commuting time, or lunch. These activities generally take a minimum of 2 to 3 hours a day.

To achieve gross billable hours of 8.5 a day, most attorneys must devote at least 10 to 12 hours per day in their practice. While there is widespread skepticism among nonlawyers about whether attorneys *actually* spend 60 hours a week in their offices, this is not unusual. Whether the time in the office is *efficiently* spent is another matter.

There are, of course, other ways of achieving "minimum" time. Double and even triple billing is one of them. For example, assume an attorney has two cases pending involving similar matters of law. The attorney researches the issue and prepares a memorandum on the subject. Since the research is equally applicable to both clients, some attorneys feel justified in billing *each* of them for the research time. This is rationalized under the theory that if only *one* client had been responsible for it, that client would have paid the full amount anyway.

In the above example, if it took six hours to research and prepare the memo, the attorney could log twelve "billable" hours on his time sheets and take off the rest of the day. This practice is particularly prevalent in "macho" law firms, which regard extraordinary billable hours as a symbol of industriousness.

Yearly loggings of 3,000, and even 3,500, hours are not unheard of, and 2,500 gross billable hours is the norm in many firms with high testosterone levels. Mathematicians might well ask how it is possible to bill 3,500 hours in a given year. That represents over 9 billable hours a day, 365 days a year. It also assumes that an attorney never takes a single holiday, never gets sick, and works at least 12 to 13 hours a day to achieve this goal.

To suggest that this strains credulity would be an understatement. About the only way this can be done is through double billing. While the attorney's justification for double billing may pass the "blush" test among other lawyers (it is hard to embarrass a lawyer), clients should be disturbed for a few reasons.

First, clients hire counsel based on their expectation that an attorney is expert in a field. While even the best lawyers need to do specialized research on close questions, expertise is supposed to be reflected in an attorney's hourly rates.

Second, if the attorney's rationalization of "double billing" is ethically defensible, another practice would also be acceptable—billing Client A for research done on behalf of Client B five years ago. Indeed, a memorandum on a particular point of law could have an almost infinite value in that the research could be billed over and over again. Although this is not a common practice, it is not inconceivable, since most major firms maintain "Memo Files" which are carefully cross-indexed.

Lawyers also use a number of other contrivances to reach their billable hour goals. Among these are the following:

Retainer Clients. Some clients choose to pay a law firm a fixed annual fee to have the firm represent them on *all* their matters. While some clients believe that retainers will induce the attorneys to work as little as possible on their matters so as to maximize the law firm's profitability, this is rarely the case in firms which have a minimum gross-billable-hours standard. Since retainer clients rarely question the number of hours spent on a matter, lawyers tend to load time sheets with hours for retainer clients thus increasing their gross billable hours.

The argument here is that, "[t]here is no harm done to the client, therefore, it is ethical." While this argument might pass scrutiny of clients, it inherently camouflages the inefficiency of a law firm. This is the same type of mechanism used by the Minsk Bicycle Factory in the bad old days of the Evil Empire and explains why Minsk is having a tough time competing in a free market.

Contingent Fees. Contingent fees are often defended by lawyers as a mechanism to provide legal services to those who cannot afford it. In these cases, the law firm agrees to work for a fixed percentage of damages but collect their fees only if they are successful in getting a monetary recovery from a defendant.

In these circumstances, attorneys are motivated to put as many hours as possible into the contingent fee matter, since they are not technically being paid by the hour. The "net realized hourly rate," (the recovery divided by the number of hours), declines the more work is done and is inherently inefficient. Nevertheless, "larding" contingent fee cases with hours provides a good "sump" for an attorney to reach the gross billable hour goals established by the firm.

Punitive Damage Cases. The real gold mine for attorneys wishing to maximize their gross billable hours is in cases involving punitive damages (especially against wealthy corporate defendants). In these cases, plaintiffs (who are sometimes grouped in a class action, involving thousands of individual claims against a manufacturer, insurer, airline, or other deep-pockets company) do not pay anything to their lawyers. If the attorneys are successful in achieving recovery from the defendant, and the defendant's conduct is demonstrated to have been willful or grossly negligent (or in the case of certain products, such as pharmaceuticals, inadvertent), the attorneys stand to collect their fees from the defendant directly.

During the course of litigation, the defendant has *no* opportunity to review or object to the amount of fees or hours worked by plaintiffs' lawyers. It is only at the end of a case when the judge reviews the reasonableness of fees that the defendants can protest.

Even here fees are usually granted by the court in that the attorneys' fees are presented as an additional punishment to the defendant for his misdeeds.

Such awards of attorneys' fees can often exceed the *entire* monetary damages awarded to the plaintiffs, and law firms often throw platoons of associates into prosecuting these claims. Hours logged by lawyers in punitive damage cases can make the most industrious Korean salaryman look indolent by comparison.

"It is the trade of lawyers to question every-thing, yield nothing, and talk by the hour."

Thomas Jefferson

CHAPTER 3

Hourly Rates

"The hourly rate is not a great arrangement... It seems to me that you are always better off in a fixed fee arrangement."—Thomas Decker, vice-president /general counsel/secretary, CertainTeed Corporation and Norton Company, *American Lawyer*, June 1992.

By the late 1980s, most lawyers in the United States charged for services based on an hourly basis, the same way bricklayers and hamburger flippers do. This system developed over decades (in part, due to complaints by clients that lawyers' charges were too high). In the nineteenth and early twentieth centuries, lawyers routinely billed their clients relatively standard fees based upon their experience in performing a particular service. For example, a simple will might cost $50 at the turn of the century; an uncontested divorce, $200; and, a house closing, $100.

Some clients, however, complained that such fixed rates led to price fixing and extraordinarily high hourly rates for some lawyers. For their part, lawyers responded with a Br'er Rabbit defense. "Please, oh, please," they pleaded, "don't throw us into that briar patch of hourly rates. Oh, nooooo!" Citing the concern over price fixing charges, they agreed to hourly rates as a standard for the industry and touted it as a consumer-protection measure. The result has been a disaster for clients.

Hourly rates now guarantee that clients will be overcharged for almost any conceivable legal service and is one of the most anticompetitive aspects of the legal profession.

For their part, lawyers also closely track studies that have found attorneys who keep track of their time earn more than lawyers who do not. The message was that lawyers who kept track of their time tended to have a better idea of their cost of doing business. But the message was misinterpreted to mean that if lawyers billed by the hour, they made more money. And, as computers became available to keep track of time and produce bills, hourly billing became the standard method.

The concept of value to the client was totally lost. Lawyers persuaded clients that the only reasonable basis for billing should be the effort made on the client's behalf. Through time records, lawyers could objectively prove what had been done for the client. Once clients were "trained" to expect such an "objective" standard for billing, compensation decisions within the firm also began to be based more on production—billable hours—than on the value produced.

Hourly rates vary from city to city and from firm to firm but have little to do with the quality of legal services being offered. They have much more to do with the overhead of larger firms and what they can get away with. Many clients, particularly corporate executives, believe as an article of faith that (a) to get good legal advice one needs to go to a large firm, and (b) the quality of legal service is directly proportionate to what is paid for it—a myth eagerly embraced by much of the legal profession.

In fact, legal fees are driven by (a) "reverse competition," (b) preservation of the myth of price-driven quality, and (c) the fact that the larger the firm gets, the less it is inclined to operate efficiently and must increase its prices to cover its costs.

Hourly fees vary enormously. Some firms charge as little as $40 an hour for a junior associate, others $600 an hour or more for senior partners. Does the market control these fees? Only partly. The reverse competition of hourly rates suggests that a firm will charge as much as it can depending upon how much its *competitors* are able to get away with. Thus, if Firm A wants to maximize its gross income by increasing its hourly rate $15 an hour across the board, Firm B feels almost compelled to match this increase.

This is much like pricing in the liquor industry. Sometimes sales are inversely proportionate to the price charged. A rise in the price of a brand of Scotch, for example, may actually *increase* sales as it gains snob appeal, while reducing prices may undercut the image of the brand as a quality product.

Although there are certainly differences in skill levels among law firms and individual lawyers, the quality of legal services offered by a particular lawyer has less to do with that individual's skills than the snob appeal of the firm for which the individual is working. It is not unusual for a lawyer to move from one firm to another, and add $40 an hour to his hourly billing rate, merely because the firm to which the attorney migrates is based in a city with high rates.

Hourly rates are generally set by reference to what the firm perceives to be its primary competition and will raise its fees to the maximum extent possible. Lowering hourly rates is regarded as passé and may actually reduce the attractiveness of the firm to big-ticket clients. The price of legal services has little relationship to the value to the client but rather to the law firm itself. Maximizing the income of the firm is the primary objective, not delivering legal services.

Setting hourly rates in most major firms also genuflects to the marketplace. Firms are fond of sending notices to clients at the beginning of each year announcing their new rates and claiming that they are in line with inflation. This is designed to convince the client that the rate increases are reasonable. Nevertheless, if a lawyer in a metropolitan area who charges $500 a hour raises her rates by the rate of inflation (say, 8 percent or $40) to $540 an hour and another lawyer in a rural area raises her rate from $120 to $130 (a $10 increase), is the metropolitan lawyer going to deliver $30 more justice or service?

Hourly rates have little to do with inflation or quality; they have *everything* to do with enabling law firms to maximize their income, both through manipulation of the hourly rates and the way these hourly rates are used.

CHAPTER 4

The Hours Opiate

"Of course, almost all firms have stated policies that forbid...unethical and illegal billing practices. The extent to which these policies are actually followed depends on the firm culture, on the unspoken messages that the leaders of the firm send to its lawyers."—Seth Rosner, *American Bar Association Journal*, May 1992.

The emphasis on gross billable hours by law firms is unfair to clients, raises legal fees, and magnifies the current earnings of major law firms. Will it take a head-on confrontation between clients and their counsel to abolish this system? Not necessarily. The gross billable hours standard is just as destructive to the firms adopting it as it is to the clients upon whom it is imposed.

Because a gross billable hour measure of performance rewards inefficiency and penalizes competence, firms that embrace this standard sow the seeds of their own demise.

As a practical matter, the gross billable hours standard has several immediate effects on a law firm.

Cooking the Books

Most major law firms have computerized "back rooms." These back rooms are primarily responsible for computing hourly charges to clients. During the workday, attorneys fill out time logs listing the client, the matter, a brief description of the services performed, and how long it took the attorney to perform these services. Most law firms insist on one-tenth hour or one-quarter hour increments. That is, every task that a lawyer undertakes will be billed at least 6 minutes and, in many firms, up to 15 minutes. A lawyer whose hourly billing rate is $240 an hour, then, is thus billing the equivalent of $4 per minute. A two-minute telephone call can result in client charges of $24, if the attorney is on a one-tenth hour increment system, or $60, if on the one-quarter hour increment system.

This is one way that a lawyer can bill 10 or more hours in an 8-hour day. If a lawyer makes as many as 5 telephone calls per hour, for example, that can mean 5 one-quarter hour increments in 60 minutes! The "business office" in law firms does not usually challenge hours that attorneys log on their time sheets; their responsibility is only to reduce these to computerized formats.

Generally, clients are assigned a file and billing number for their matter. The descriptions provided by the attorneys are entered into the computer and, at the end of every billing cycle, a statement is generated listing all of the matters and time, together with the descriptions for the client's monthly statement.

In most major law firms, a "prebill" is then given to the billing partner (the attorney assigned to review statements going to the client). A billing partner will have authority to adjust the bill either up or down within limits established by the firm. Usually these limits are denominated in dollars. That is, the billing partner will have the authority to adjust the statement up or down (a process commonly referred to a "write-ups" or "write-offs") within a certain dollar limit. This authority is usually discretionary, and varies from firm to firm .

Some billing partners use this discretion to write up a bill on the basis of his perception as to the value of services rendered. In this case, the billing partner will add hours to the prebill if, in his judgment the client will pay for it and the matter was worth more than the preliminary gross billable hours would indicate. These write-ups are penciled in by the attorney, corrected by the business office, and included in the final statement for that billing cycle.

Other attorneys may write down, or entirely write off, a bill if the attorney believes the client would either be unable to pay or that the gross billable time marked on the prebill is excessive. This is often a difficult call and raises another question. If an attorney believes the time spent was excessive given the work that was done, why wasn't he able to determine what a reasonable amount was before the work was undertaken in the first place?

Given the fact that associates are encouraged to bill as many hours as possible, write-downs are relatively common. They are, however, discouraged in firms that focus on gross billable hours, in that this represents money out of the partners' pockets.

Depending upon the sophistication of the firm's business (or accounting) office, write-downs are easier than might be suspected. If the write-downs are not reflected in the gross billable hours initially submitted by an attorney (that is, if the written-off hours are not deducted from the gross billable hours), the attorney in question may still get credit for working hard without any penalty for his inefficiency. Other, more sophisticated firms, have computer programs which will track the "net realized" hours of all attorneys which deduct write-offs from the gross billable hours. In these cases, there is even less motivation for a billing partner to write down or write off hours for either the partner, or any of the associates working for her, in that it will reflect poorly on her chances for advancement.

The billing partner is less likely to write off her own hours, even if she wants to make adjustments to an excessive bill. The billing partner has the power to write off another attorney's hours on the assumption that they were inefficient. Guess whose hours get written off first?

This system builds in an enormous amount of resentment among attorneys who are subject to the whims of the billing partner. If the firm has a sophisticated computer system that tracks "net realized" hours, an entire career can be wrecked by having the billing partner write off hours of another partner or associate as being inefficient.

After the corrected bills have been returned to the business office, they are reprogrammed in the computer and returned to the billing partner for submission to the client. Generally, a final statement for the current billing cycle will be sent to the client with a standard cover letter from the billing partner. If, after receiving the bill, the client questions certain items, it is generally the prerogative of the billing partner to further write down contested amounts. It is rare that a partner will have an opportunity to write up a bill once it is submitted. The client is already protesting the amount charged.

Writing down of "accounts receivable" is a common practice, especially with large, established clients. A challenge of $2,000 to $3,000 by a client who is paying $100,000 a year, usually is within the discretion of the billing partner. Larger write offs may have to be referred to a firm committee for approval. As is the case with the prebills, firms handle these accounts receivable write-offs in different ways.

In some firms, gross billable hours submitted by the originating attorney are unaffected; the attorney will get credit for the work done, even if it is written off by the billing partner due to a challenge by the client. In other firms, challenges from clients resulting in a write-off of an account receivable are deducted from the hours originally submitted by an attorney. In these firms, a client's ability to get adjustments is more difficult than in firms where attorneys are not penalized for their inefficiency. Nevertheless, the pressure to maintain a "net realized" rate close to the gross rate in large firms is intense, and overcharges are stoutly (if incredibly) defended.

Kudos to Bart Simpson

The gross billable hours standard rewards incompetence and indolence. Assume a law firm hires two lawyers from the same law school class, and both are given equivalent assignments their first year. Lawyer A is, shall we say, a perfectly nice person but rather lazy and not particularly bright. Lawyer B, however, is not only a hard worker but is a quick study, able to spot legal issues and resolve them in a minimum time.

On equivalently difficult matters, Lawyer A consistently takes 100 hours to come up with a workmanlike product. A has researched the law, gone through seven or eight drafts, and finally produced a competent 10-page memo, appropriately footnoted.

Lawyer B spots the legal issues immediately, dictates a draft to her secretary, makes minor modifications, and produces a draft equivalent to that of A in only 50 hours. Both have produced the same result, but who has performed the greater service to the client? If both A and B are billed at the same hourly rate, Lawyer B is the runaway champion, from a client's perspective.

Under the gross billable hours standard however, Lawyer A, the indolent dullard, is the hero to the law firm. This truism is not lost on associates.

All work is "dumbed down" to the lowest possible common denominator. Even the brightest attorney will maximize her hours—not to serve clients—but so as not to make her colleagues look bad, as well as the practical goal of making herself look good.

Clients suffer in this equation. They have little way of telling who is a "good" or "bad" attorney, since the really good ones will "fake it," perversely attempting to demonstrate that they are not as good as they really are. Many of the very brightest lawyers, in fact, leave the practice of law entirely when they see their chances of progress barred by their intellectual inferiors.

It is not unusual in large law firms to find senior partners who lack any spark of originality, much less genius, making handsome salaries while others of both superior intellect and diligence are far below them in compensation. This hierarchy is introduced even in law school.

Law schools in the United States, by and large, are not designed to reward intellectual curiosity and insight, but rather "hard slogging." The best law students are often not those who have an understanding of the law and can accomplish things quickly but rather those who demonstrate a willingness to "tote the barge and lift the bale."

Nevertheless, given the attractiveness of the law as a career, tens of thousands of very smart rabbits are admitted to the bar every year and, almost miraculously, some actually succeed in becoming leaders of their profession. However, given the fact that the highest rewards in law firms go to Bart Simpson-like underachievers, mediocrity, indolence, and incompetence are often more amply rewarded than brilliance.

Many attorneys will bridle at the suggestion that they are "indolent." In their defense, they will cite the thousands of hours they spend in the office each year, on the road, and even in the shower, thinking about clients' matters—and produce reams of time sheets to demonstrate their beaverlike addiction to hard work. Even putting aside the manner in which many lawyers "cook the books," there is a fundamental difference between working *long* and working *hard*.

All of us are familiar with construction crews, many of whose members are paid extraordinary hourly rates for propping up a shovel or making sure a wall does not fall down by leaning against it while smoking a cigarette. Since attorneys in firms with the gross billable hours rule are motivated to take as long as possible on any given project, working *hard* (and efficiently) on that project is self-defeating.

Almost any excuse to lengthen the time necessary to accomplish a project is rewarded if it can be demonstrated to have any relevance to the matter at hand. Even reading a daily newspaper can be justified in that the attorney has to maintain a knowledge about the world at large, and perusing a trade newspaper in the client's field of endeavor is more often than not billed as research time, necessary to enhance the attorney's ability to service the client.

While it is undoubtedly true that familiarity with clients' needs and business is useful, it is questionable whether the client should pay an attorney to gain knowledge that the client has a right to expect in any event. While an attorney may cite the fact that he has devoted thousands of hours to a particular project, the inefficiencies demanded by the gross billable hours standard predispose most attorneys to be indolent in the common under-standing of the term.

CHAPTER 5

Research Time

Research time is the sinkhole of gross billable hours. This is the most subjective part of any lawyer's bill.

In the Anglo-Saxon legal tradition, prior court decisions may bind subsequent courts in their interpretation of the law. This is extremely complex. Despite 200 years of experience, each case presents unique facts which must be interpreted *vis-a-vis* both the statutory law (which is often vague) and cases which *interpret* that law. This is what most legal disputes are all about. Legal research is essential in almost any legal action. Most law firms have libraries in which lawyers can refer to cases proving their points; they research prior decisions attempting to show that the law should be interpreted in a particular way.

In the last fifteen years, lawyers have increasingly relied upon electronic databases to assist them in legal research. These databases have millions of documents which can be accessed by attorneys using their personal computers. A legal proceeding may involve hundreds of issues. Depending upon the complexity of the case and the seriousness of the outcome, lawyers may research some, or all, of the issues. This is an enormously time-consuming process. Precedents must not only be identified but "Shepardized." That is, the lawyer must determine if the decision upon which he is going to base his argument is the most recent and has not been overturned, or modified, by subsequent decisions.

The Red Herring Rule

As noted above, in a given legal proceeding, there are generally many issues. The lawyer's first objective is to identify the issues relevant to the case. This is one of the best examples of where a lawyer's expertise and experience come to play.

Highly skilled counsel will be able to determine relatively quickly what the major issues are and focus their research on those matters. Less-experienced counsel generally can find the big issues but may also identify issues that are not really problems at all. They spend enormous amounts of time "proving the negative." That is, demonstrating that some issues are really red herrings, with no relevance to the outcome of the legal proceeding. It is not unusual for a substantial amount of time spent chasing shadows to be billed to a client.

This is particularly true in firms that emphasize gross billable hours. In the name of thoroughness, an attorney can justify hundreds of hours in front of a video monitor searching for problems which do not exist. They can justify this on their bill by noting that if the problem *did* exist, it could affect the outcome of the proceeding. Even experienced counsel are inclined to undertake unnecessary research since it looks good on their billing sheets, and they can justify it as the highest form of professionalism, in that they have left no stone unturned.

This is similar to a physician ordering an expensive CAT scan of a patient's cranium when the patient has injured his big toe, "just to be on the safe side." The descriptions of research time in most lawyers' time sheets are also marvelously vague. Notations such as "research *re* Constitutional issues" are common. Statements often do not describe exactly which constitutional issues are being researched, what the outcome was, or if the attorney concluded that it was a red herring. The client has no way of knowing whether the research was justified.

Breaking the Habit

Adequate research is so subjective that it borders on theology—on the wrong side of the border. Firms that emphasize gross billable hours also emphasize research, to the point it approaches a Zen mantra. Every hour spent in the library or via microchip increases gross billable hours. Research can become infinite, particularly in cases involving complex litigation where almost every comma can be researched *ad infinitum*. This is the purest form of heroin for a law firm—but the client gets to pay the bill.

The gross billable hours opiate has been in place for so long it will be a difficult habit to break. Rewarding inefficiency, confusing production with productivity, and measuring competence in terms of an ability to pass along higher costs to consumers will ultimately be destructive when law firms are forced to meet free-market competition. Law firms will be required to go through the same catharsis that Eastern European factories have once the free-market system catches up to the legal community.

"A man may as well open an oyster without a knife as a lawyer's mouth without a fee."

Barton Holyday

CHAPTER 6

Making Virtue of Vice

"One challenge of negotiating [the] flat fee arrangements will be to determine—in advance— the scope of service the fee covers, and the charges for any work beyond that scope. In addition, where bonuses are tied to the outcome of a case, lawyer and client must agree on which results qualify for a bonus. For instance, a client may tell [a lawyer] that result A is great, result B is acceptable, and result C is terrible. So if a case goes to trial, as do most cases, [many lawyers] handle—and if he wins a slam-dunk defense verdict, he might earn a happy bonus. If the plaintiff wins a verdict but falls below the settlement demand, the bonus would drop. If the case bombs with a verdict higher than what the defense could have settled for, no bonus...

> *"Of course, clients like Henry Pearce, General Counsel of General Motors, are providing new incentives [to lawyers] 'it's a whole new approach in the way any law firm is representing us in cases,' says Pearce. 'I'd like to see [this] initiative replicated...if [lawyers] can demonstrate what I believe they can demonstrate, we will absolutely give them more volume.'"—The American Lawyer*, May 1992, page 5.

Many lawyers will protest that whatever vices are nourished by the gross billable hours standard, the very nature of legal work leaves them with few realistic alternatives and that billing by the hour is the only fair way to compensate themselves and provide legal services. They point out the following:

1. Complexity. Fixing a legal problem is not like repairing a car. Every problem is unique. While a simple will may require only a few hours, a client may require a much more complex document if they have specific needs. Further, legal problems can have many solutions; each one must be approached individually. At the beginning of a legal matter, particularly in the case of lawsuits or criminal defense work, lawyers know very little about how complex a case will become. Hundreds of facts are unknown, and the lawyer does not know how difficult it will be to find these facts. This is done during the course of "discovery," in which the opposite side is required to turn over documents and allow witnesses to be deposed (i.e., interrogated in the lawyer's office, under oath). This can be enormously expensive. Many attorneys argue that it is impossible to estimate the length of time it will take to complete the case until the facts, and the law, are thoroughly researched. Thus, they protest, what may appear to be a very simple matter can metastasize into a complex proceeding with new defenses appearing every day as additional facts are uncovered.

The time necessary to complete a legal proceeding is also dependent upon the vigor with which the opposition defends itself. If the other side in a lawsuit hires competent counsel, they may file numerous motions which can slow the process and increase the cost. These tactics are unknown at the beginning of a case, which makes estimating costs difficult.

Many lawyers argue that billing on an hourly basis is really the only way to go. Since they cannot estimate how much time it will take due to "unknowns," they prefer to take it "one day at a time," throwing whatever resources appear to be necessary at the problem.

2. Availability of Resources. Since lawyers can't tell how complex a case will be when presented with the initial problem, they don't know how many resources will be required to resolve it. Even the largest law firms allocate attorneys to various projects, and most lawyers don't know what projects they will be working on one month hence.

The attorney to whom you initially explain your matter may not have the slightest idea what other attorneys may be requested to assist in the prosecution of the case. Since lawyers' hourly rates vary greatly, and a lawyer will tell you that he cannot know what technical assistance he may need, it is difficult for him to give you estimates of costs up-front.

While all of the above objections are somewhat legitimate, clients should not be intimidated. Competent counsel should be able to give you an estimate of the time necessary to accomplish your objective. Surely, the discovery process has many unknowables, but lawyers who have had experience in a particular field should be able to anticipate these and build them into a fee. The more competent the lawyer is in a particular field, the more he will be able to anticipate what problems will arise and build that into an estimate.

Consumers of legal services should search for the most competent counsel who have experience in a given field of law and who know what kinds of bear traps are out there.

Insist on a Budget

One method of determining how confident a lawyer is in his own abilities is to insist that he prepare a budget before a case starts and make a commitment to stick to it. This process will tell you three things about the lawyer:

1. The lawyer and the law firm will do everything possible to work efficiently so as not to exceed their budgets.

2. A lawyer is confident of his own abilities in the field and is comfortable with his estimate. If he is BSing you, he is only fooling himself.

3. The lawyer will have many sleepless nights worrying about whether he will be able to make his budget. That is generally a good thing (for a client). There are those who contend that this system would encourage lawyers to cut corners. A cynic would respond that they do so anyway but charge you for it. Cynic A would tell you that. Realist B would suggest that many corners *ought* to be cut in the interest of efficiency. Walking around the park is not necessarily better than following the diagonal sidewalk to opposite corner.

For all the protests by lawyers that they simply cannot know what a case will involve, that is precisely what you are paying them for. Competent, experienced counsel will generally know what to expect and how much it will cost to do it.

One note of caution—requesting bids up-front will generally yield a higher estimate of cost than if you did not insist upon this. Don't be overly concerned. The budget costs will almost certainly be below that which you would have spent on a gross billable hours system since costs in the latter system are open ended. It is not only common but ubiquitous that gross billable hours law firms give low-ball estimates to clients so long as they are not held to them. They then inflate the price as the case goes along, until the final bill approaches the national debt of Nicaragua. Clients are almost always better served by having a firm figure up-front.

Even though you may need to take smelling salts before you open the envelope with the bid, realize that you truly are better off having a fixed number that you can live with than be ambushed during the course of litigation by recurrent bills.

Many clients, burned by high legal fees, seek to negotiate a reduction of those fees "after the fact." This almost always leads to disputes and lack of trust between attorneys and their clients. It is far better to negotiate *before* requesting legal services. Here are some of the things you can do:

1. Request a negotiated fee. If an attorney refuses to negotiate a fee, hire another lawyer.

2. Ask for a "cap" on fees. Many law firms will agree to a cap on fees for a particular matter. This is not always the case (particularly in litigation), but even there, it is a useful milestone for reviewing what has been done and what needs to be done.

3. Agree to contingencies or partial contingencies. Many matters can be handled on a "contingency basis" that is, if you win, the lawyer gets paid; if he loses, he does not. Often, however, "contingency fees" are not reasonable, and you will find *no* lawyer who will accept them. In these cases, however, you might request that the lawyer set a partial contingency. That is, if he succeeds in a particular commercial dispute, for example, that you will pay him his regular hourly fees plus a bonus of X percent, but if he loses, his regularly hourly fees will be discounted by Y percent. Most lawyers are in the business of practicing *law* and have limited appreciation for a commercial risk. Therefore, asking your lawyer to accept a percentage of your increased income (or decreased liability) based upon his success or failure in litigation is not reasonable.

CHAPTER 7

Bundling and Unbundling

"When money becomes the primary goal, a law firm may end up choosing to systematically and deliberately inflate client bills and even to bill for expenses not actually incurred for those clients."
—Seth Rosner, *American Bar Association Journal*, May 1992.

Throughout most of the twentieth century, it has been common for law firms to charge clients for direct out-of-pocket expenses. These have traditionally included postage, long-distance telephone calls, travel expenses, filing fees, and photocopying fees. Most other overhead costs of a lawyer were "bundled" into the lawyer's hourly rate. That is, the overhead costs of running a law firm (for example, secretarial salaries, office equipment, supplies, and library costs) were paid for by the lawyer at no additional charge to the client. The lawyer's hourly rate may have appeared high, but overhead costs often accounted for 50 percent or more of the total cost of running a law firm.

As the 1970s approached, however, law firms started to "unbundle" some of these costs and pass them directly to clients. It is no longer unusual to see the following expenses billed to clients.

- Computer time
- Secretarial overtime
- Messenger services
- Photocopying
- Local telephone charges
- Book-binding fees

the list goes on and on.

In some major firms, even coffee and doughnuts supplied by the firm's own caterers are billed to clients under various guises ("provisions," "commissary").

While there could be a reasonable debate concerning the justification of passing along extraordinary printing costs, many lawyers would be hard pressed to justify many other costs that have been unbundled, particularly given their extraordinarily high hourly billing rates.

Computer Time

"The current system of hourly billing provides a definite disincentive for using technology. Since lawyers are paid according to the hours worked, it usually is more profitable to complete a routine task from 'scratch,' and spend 20 hours doing it, rather than to enter the basic document on a computer and spend only one hour to adapt it to the matter at hand."

A common billing category, computer research time, generally relates to the time spent by lawyers and legal assistants on such on-line legal research services as Lexis®, or Westlaw®. These services are available in most major law firms, and lawyers can link on to the service by modems. Charges for these services range from $50 to $300 an hour depending upon the nature of the search.

Since the costs of computer research are often passed on directly to the client, lawyers have no motivation to keep their on-line time to a minimum. In fact, poorly trained lawyers often spend hours on computer research that could be effectively done by legal assistants in a fraction of the time. This not only maximizes the unbundled computer research charges, but the client also pays the higher rates for an experienced lawyer.

While in former times it would have been unusual for a law firm to bill clients directly for library costs, the computer has taken the place of the law library as the primary research tool of many lawyers. This has resulted in an explosion of legal research fees borne by clients not only for the time spent in research but the cost of the materials as well—even *before* the lawyer's hourly rates are factored in.

Some lawyers justify unbundling of computer research time under the guise that it actually costs the client less because computers can be more efficient and search a greater body of law than is available in almost any law library. This is true but misses the point. Although computers enable counsel to achieve results more quickly and efficiently, the net effect has *not* been to reduce legal fees but to increase them. This is not the fault of the technology but rather the manner in which it is billed by law firms. For their part, computer service firms know that most lawyers pass these costs on to clients and are not motivated to reduce their fees. Lawyers do not demand lower computer costs, so the only winners are the computer service companies and the lawyers they serve. Clients are the losers.

Photocopying

In most law firms, the photocopying room is a profit center. Although industrial-strength copying machines can be expensive, this cost can be quickly amortized by charging clients a fixed amount per page. Such charges have been facilitated in the last decade by sophisticated programmable computers attached to the copying machine which allows each copying job to be directly billed to the client's "out-of-pocket expense" account.

While some clients have extraordinary copying demands (for example, massive duplication of documents requested during the course of litigation), clients rarely know what is being printed in a law firm's photocopying center. In many cases, dozens of drafts are photocopied, notations made on alternate pages, and the old version dumped in the recycling bin. Nevertheless, clients are charged $.07 to $.30 a page for each draft.

This can run up an out-of-pocket expense tab in unbundled photocopying fees, with no effective way for a client to gauge whether these costs are necessary. Since the law firm has no motivation to reduce photocopying (in fact, it has every motivation to increase it since it makes a profit on every page produced), it is in its interest to sacrifice forests of trees to the copying machines at the expense of the client.

In the mid-1970s, we were promised a "paperless" office by the year 2000. Alas, this is not to be. The insatiable photocopier, propelled by open-ended billings, guarantees that substantially *more* paper will be consumed by the turn of the century due to the economics of unbundled billing.

Messenger Services

Messenger service is another example of unbundling. Most larger firms hire general-purpose employees to run the photocopying machines, move furniture, and deliver messages. These vary from formal filings with a court to correspondence with the client or counsel down the street. Since most larger cities have commercial messenger services, law firms feel justified in using their *own* messengers and charging commercial rates. This applies to such tasks as taking a bag of mail to the post office.

While there are times when the use of a messenger is necessary (for example, taking a five-pound package across town), given the fact that this is an unbundled cost, law firms regard messengers as a profit center. In some firms, the entire cost of office help can be covered by messenger services. Rather than have office help sitting in the back room reading a newspaper, law firms have a self-interest in making sure they are gainfully employed by delivering messages, whether necessary or not, since these costs can be passed directly to clients.

Another ploy some law firms use to maximize income from messengers is to have them make daily runs to various destinations around town—much like a mail route—picking up and delivering routine documents along the way. Multiple clients can be billed for the same trip, whether or not any of the documents in question required the service of a messenger.

Facsimile Transmissions

Firms also capitalize on other means of transmitting information. It is not unusual for a client to receive unbundled charges for facsimile transmissions. Like copying machines, computer technology permits a firm to program sophisticated fax machines to list all outgoing faxes by client, whether across the street or around the world. Fax charges of a dollar a page, or more, are common (in addition to the phone charges). A simple two-page letter from Lawyer A to Lawyer B three blocks away can result in unbundled charges (not including the lawyer's fee for preparing the letter) as follows:

Word processing charges	$ 7.00
Duplication	2.00
Fax transmission	3.00
Total:	$12.00

In many firms, these charges would be unbundled and passed on to the client.

Word Processing

"Word processing" is a term used to cover a multitude of sins in law firms. In prior years, law firms captured the costs of their office equipment in their hourly charges. Not so in the late twentieth century. In word-processing centers where trolls toil in the glare of cathode ray tubes, law firms have found a source of additional profit.

Most firms are equipped with state-of-the-art computer technology which enables any lawyer to draft documents. For certain matters, this becomes tedious; some lawyers prefer to dictate rather than type their own documents. These tasks have been consigned to the word-processing centers. In these dungeons, scribes key in lengthy transcripts, put documents into Desktop Publishing format, scan documents into computers, and correct lengthy drafts.

In most word-processing centers, the equipment is not much different than that used by the lawyers, but generally, word processors are skilled typists. They have a good feel for their equipment and can produce documents more efficiently and quickly than lawyers.

This gain in efficiency would, however, cut into a law firm's income, so firms rely on another ploy: if efficiency would reduce earnings, then charge clients for the increased efficiency by passing these differences along in unbundled costs. This is usually done in the form of a word-processing charge, which can be expressed either as a function of the number of pages produced or at an hourly rate (generally between $10 and $30 per hour).

Here, again, clients are expected to pay for basic overhead costs of the law firm, in addition to the lawyer's hourly rates.

While most word-processing centers are not as lucrative as duplication rooms, clients pay part of the cost of overhead for the law firm, thus increasing the firm's profitability.

This also has the perverse effect of encouraging lawyers *not* to utilize the technology available to them but rather to refer documents to word processing because the charges can be passed along to the client. Abuse is not as high in this area as in others, however, since by typing a document, a lawyer can maximize hourly fees, which is more lucrative than passing it on to a (nonbillable) secretary. However, the question that remains: why should a client be expected to pay *any* secretarial costs?

Secretarial Overtime

Secretarial overtime is one of the more insidious unbundled charges. While law firms must by law pay secretaries overtime when they work beyond statutory maximums, this often is not due to the client's requirements but rather that of the law firm. Secretaries are expected to perform various duties during the course of the day, ranging from answering the phones to opening mail. If an emergency comes up at ten in the morning, the secretary may not be free to begin working on the project until four in the afternoon, and if he works until nine at night, the secretary is paid overtime.

These additional costs significantly reduce a firm's incentive to demand efficiency from their office staff. Many secretaries *want* overtime and are in a unique position to demand it as a matter of *legal* right. This creates a problem for the lawyer.

During the early 1980s, the American Corporate Counsel Association recommended that secretarial overtime be approved *in advance* by clients. Otherwise, such overtime would be absorbed by the firm. This recommendation, however, is often circumvented.

Almost by definition, emergencies require overtime secretarial help. The real question is whether the *client's* work, or routine office tasks, is being done during the overtime hours. Secretarial overtime pay charges can be eyeopening.

A senior secretary in a large firm can have a base rate of $30 an hour, and the client can pay $45 a hour to have a letter typed at six at night, when it could have been done for free at four. There are, of course, instances where secretarial overtime is clearly attributable to a client's demands. For example, when a secretary travels with an attorney to work on depositions and is in a hotel room day after day. Even here, there is no motivation for the firm to insist that the secretary work efficiently during normal working hours since all additional costs can be passed on to the client.

This problem is compounded by the habit of many attorneys not to even *inform* a secretary of client emergencies until five p.m. Even if a secretary was *not* seeking overtime, she will generally comply with the request. It is the client, of course, who pays for the attorney's oversight in failing to advise his secretary that overtime would be required. The most efficient secretary on the planet cannot prevent client overtime charges under these circumstances.

Unlike other examples of unbundling, secretarial overtime is not a significant source of additional revenue for law firms, but it does underwrite costs and provides some secretaries with an attractive salary. In fact, most law firms value proficient senior legal secretaries and, in addition to a reasonable annual salary (averaging around $40,000 in larger firms and in the mid-$20s for the smaller, "boutique" firms) and paid holidays, firms offer their secretaries benefit packages which can include up to three weeks of paid vacation leave, ten days paid sick leave, paid or employer-assisted medical and dental benefits, and 401(k) retirement or IRA accounts.

It is not unusual for a secretary's base hours to be around 1,500 a year at $30 an hour and for her to work another 100 hours a year in overtime at $45 an hour. A tidy sum, a portion of which can be passed along to clients. Whether a senior legal secretary is worth $45,000 a year is a matter of some dispute, except to the lawyer who values her services, but clients are in no position to argue about the value of the secretary to her lawyer even though they pay for a portion of it directly.

Travel

> *"If a lawyer must travel first class for his or her ego, then let him or her pick up the difference between business class or coach and first class."*—John Ogden, general counsel/secretary/contract management director, Werner & Pfleiderer Corporation, *American Lawyer*, 1992.

Lawyers often travel like oil sheiks—if it is at the clients' expense. The Concorde between New York and London is generally half filled with attorneys who booked their tickets at the last minute. Their travel costs are enough to buy a starter house in Minneapolis.

Law firms generally have two sets of travel rules. One for travel at firm expense, another if the client is picking up the tab. Usually, a law firm's internal travel expense policies are moderate. Large, geographically dispersed firms often have meetings that require the attendance of out-of-town lawyers. In these cases, attorneys are told to purchase modestly priced tickets well in advance to take advantage of airline discounts.

Not so when travel is done at the client's initiative. Here, lawyers will travel at the highest grade they can get away with and routinely purchase tickets at full retail. Airlines love them.

Lawyers are also fond of traveling since they can acquire frequent flyer miles, particularly if they fly business class or better, where they get several multiples of their miles. Some firms even suggest that lawyers use frequent flyer miles gained at the clients' expense for their internal firm travel.

It is true that much of the travel that lawyers do is unpredictable and that high-priced fares come with the territory. Nevertheless, there are many times a lawyer knows a month in advance that he must travel (to annual conventions, court dates, etc.). Reduced fares are available, yet lawyers rarely take advantage of them.

Telecommunications

> *"We're probably seeing mark ps in various bills and are assuming that it's just a dollar-for-dollar charge. We're starting to look closer."*—James Pricarico, Jr.,

managing deputy/general counsel/senior vice-
president, Prudential Securities, *American Lawyer*,
June 1992.

Telecommunications are another area of unbundling. As communications technology has improved, many law firms have signed
contracts with "alternative" telecommunications companies, paying a flat monthly fee plus modest increments for usage. The communications companies like these arrangements since they are
paid whether the lines are used or not. Law firms like them, too,
since they can charge full rates for the use of a low-priced lines
for long distance calls.

While most would agree that long distance (particularly
international) calls should be unbundled, charges for "tie lines"
are insidious in two respects. First, tie-line charges are sometimes not linked to the actual cost of the firm but rather to an
arbitrary fee negotiated by the firm and its long distance carrier. It is rare that a firm will give explicit breakdowns of tie-
line charges, in that it would reveal the extraordinary savings
that the firm makes on these charges but which are not passed
along to the client .

For large firms, tie-line charges are sometimes camouflaged
in long distance charges but are not backed up with actual
invoices. Tie lines can result in net profits of more than 50 percent for some firms which charge a flat rate for long distance calls,
no matter how much they are actually charged by the carrier. This,
again, serves to make the client the party responsible for the overhead costs of the law firm and encourages lawyers to make unnec-

essary telephone charges; every time a telephone call is made, it is another dollar in the lawyers' pocket.

Does cost recovery by unbundling really make any difference? Is the client going to be charged the same amount whether it's absorbed by the firm directly in the form of overhead or passed along in unbundled costs? No. Unbundling encourages law firms to act in the *least* efficient way possible and to *maximize* inefficiency. If a client is expected to pay for unnecessary expenses, there is no motivation for a law firm to cut such expenses. This is another reason law firm managers are rewarded on the basis of gross income rather than efficiency.

Unbundled charges can lead to significant unbundled income for many firms. It is not unusual for firms to have "other income" listed on their financial statements amounting to 5 to 10 percent of total income. Most of this is derived from profits from unbundled billings and amounts to hundreds of millions of dollars per year in added legal costs to consumers of legal services.

John Marquess of the Philadelphia auditing company Legalgard remembers when reviewing a bill from a San Diego law firm, he noticed a charge marked "HVAC." It turned out the firm wanted reimbursement for "heating, ventilation, and air conditioning." The auditor says such charges are "now a big item, particularly with New York firms." These firms, which tend to charge the country's highest fees, are notorious for billing clients for a pro-rata share of overhead, especially when a lawyer comes in on the weekend to work, he says. Clients should not only balk but find a new firm if such frippery appears on their bills.

"They all laid their heads together like as many lawyers when they are gettin' ready to prove that a man's heirs ain't got any right to his property."

Mark Twain

CHAPTER 8

The Curse of Consultations

One of the most horrifying images most clients have with regard to law firms is that of five lawyers sitting around a conference table discussing their matter, jackets off, sleeves rolled up. The lawyers are scrutinizing a contract. It is late at night. Two legal assistants and two secretaries hover in the background, incorporating revisions into a PC, cite-checking footnotes, and proofreading the text. The final product is a skein of turgidity—a masterwork of the legal craft.

Aside from the end product, the reason this scenario is so frightening is cost. Consider the following:

Partner A (3 hrs. @ $250/hr.)	=	$750
Partner B (3 hrs. @ $225/hr.)	=	$675
Associate C (3 hrs. @ $200/hr.)	=	$600
Associate D (3 hrs. @ $180/hr.)	=	$540
Associate E (3 hrs. @ $150/hr.)	=	$450

Paralegals F and G		
(3 hrs. @ $50/hr. each)	=	$300
Secretaries H and I (with overtime)		
(3 hrs. @ $40/hr. each)	=	$240
		$3,555

As can be seen from the above, the sound of multiple clocks running simultaneously can be deafening and breathtakingly expensive.

In most law firms, lawyers routinely consult with each other. If a client goes to Lawyer A with a legal problem, it is almost certain the client will receive advice from multiple attorneys, whether he sought such advice or not or has even met the other lawyers. Clients are often outraged when they get statements indicating that two, three, or more attorneys were consulting on their matter and that several clocks were running. The net rate in these circumstances can exceed $1,000 an hour.

Although on its face, such consultations appear to be the greatest menace to clients that law firms can inflict, this is not necessarily so. In fact, meetings among counsel can often *save* a client money and improve the quality of the final product. Whether consultations are used to gratuitously increase bills or are employed to increase efficiency and professionalism, however, is rarely evident on bills submitted to clients.

While "consulting" with colleagues may in some cases be an efficient use of time, the opportunity for abuse is obvious. Judith Bronsther of Accountability Services says that she regularly catches attorneys recording a few hours spent at a "meeting" on a given day when there is no corresponding entry from another lawyer.

In other cases, she has found wildly divergent accounts of the same encounter, with one lawyer listing an "internal conference" of two hours and the other supposed attendees recording it as four. In a recent audit of $373,000 attributed to "internal conferences" in a $2.5-million bill from a New York law firm, Ms. Bronsther says a third of them didn't match up. When she challenged the inconsistencies, the law firm reduced the bill.

In large law firms, attorneys tend to be specialized (tax, securities, contracts, real estate, international trade). Some lawyers spend their entire careers developing an expertise in just one or two laws governing their subject matter. They are, however, generally trained to recognize potential problems in other areas of the law but have no special skill in those fields.

Many legal questions require numerous specialties for their resolution. In these instances, consultation among experts can result in *less* time spent on resolving the issue. A specialist does not need to research many issues; decades of expertise can be brought to bear on a problem quickly and efficiently.

Consultations among lawyers in various disciplines can lead to increased efficiency and lower costs, if used judiciously.

Unfortunately, in firms that emphasize gross billable hours, this tendency of counsel to consult with one another can work *against* a client's interests. In these firms, attorneys are often reluctant to consult with lawyers who have greater expertise in an area than they. They would rather research areas unfamiliar to them, even though they could walk down the hall and have it resolved with a fifteen-minute conversation.

When they *do* decide to consult with other counsel, you can be sure that it will not be a short meeting. The "you scratch my back, I'll scratch yours" mentality prevails in such firms, and a question which could take an expert ten minutes to answer can easily stretch into an hour. In these circumstances, all lawyers involved have advanced their hours, and the client pays for it.

Sometimes an attorney who is "light" on gross billable hours will seek to consult with another attorney, even if he already knows the answer to the problem. This gives him an opportunity to explain the problem all over again to someone else and mark "consultations" on his time sheets. Firms emphasizing gross billable hours also encourage attorneys to invent problems that need to be solved by experts, even when these problems are surreal.

In firms emphasizing efficiency, consultations are one of the best ways to assure that the *least* possible time is spent on a problem. A client who has negotiated a price for a legal issue should either welcome, or not be bothered by, consultations that occur among counsel in that it is in the interest of the law firm itself to minimize hours. Consultations are one of the best ways of accomplishing this goal.

One of the largest issues in law firm billing is whether associates (junior attorneys) do the work or partners perform it. Since partners' hourly rates are generally much higher then associates', some clients opt (and often insist) that associates should be assigned the work on their behalf. This is sometimes a good idea;

sometimes not. For routine matters (e.g. drafting a simple will, simple residential real estate closings, etc.) you are probably better off having a "baby lawyer" doing the "grunt work." It does not require twenty-five years of expertise to draft a simple will.

If, however, your matter involves complex issues such as in a merger or acquisition, negotiation with the federal government, or a serious criminal matter, you may actually *save* money by insisting that a partner be directly involved in the day-to-day handling of the case.

A partner with fifteen years of experience in practicing in a particular area may be able to do "off the top of his head" what it would take an associate three weeks to learn. You should *not* be paying for an associates' "learning curve." For example, a partner at $350 an hour handling a complicated commercial real estate matter may be a bargain as compared with a $110 an hour junior associate who will put in ten times as many hours as a partner on the same issue.

This is a judgment call. You should meet regularly with your attorney to determine how he allocates resources. Most lawyers will tell you they will "send down" problems to the appropriate degree of expertise. This is not always true. They will "send down" matters depending upon a number of factors including availability of associates, their own schedules, and their own desire to maximize their *own* billable hours.

Partners in some firms, for example, "starve" their associates to maximize their own apparent gross billable hours which, of course, translates into greater profits if it is "slow time" in a law firm. There are no hard and fast rules with regard to allocation of work. Working with your counsel, however, you can get a feel for how they operate. If at any time you are not satisfied, raise the issue immediately with the partner preferably at the time you are consulting with him. It is always acrimonious to raise it when you receive the bill.

CHAPTER 9

The Calamity of the Computer

Walk into almost any law firm in the country today and you will find CRTs on almost everyone's desk from secretaries to the most senior partner. Law firms have adopted computerization with an alacrity second only to that of NASA.

Firms have adopted all types of computers ranging from massive mainframes to stand-alone PCs. By far the most popular system is PC-based LAN (Local Area Network). This system allows attorneys and secretaries access to word processing and data files from their own work stations. It also allows communication among the attorneys, sharing of printers, accommodation of E-mail systems, and access to on-line research services.

An entire industry has grown up that customizes LAN systems for law firms to permit hours recordation and billing to be done on the same computers.

Firms routinely spend $5,000 or more per station for state-of-the-art computer systems. Most law firm managers will tell you their firm purchased these systems in the interest of efficiency. While it is demonstrably true that computer systems could vastly improve the efficiency of law firms, for many firms this is not the case. Computer systems can actually *undermine* the profitability of a law firm, and many firms have taken steps to assure that this does not happen.

Imagine the following scenario. In 1975, the firm of Hinder, Haggle, Quibble & Delay employed eight partners, fourteen associates, twenty secretaries, three accounting clerks, and two law clerks. All written work by attorneys was either dictated by a lawyer or written in longhand on yellow legal pads. The latter was given to secretaries who transcribed it in draft form with electric typewriters. The drafts were returned to the lawyers for corrections, who made handwritten notes and returned them to the secretaries who retyped the entire document.

For longer documents, this process sometimes went back and forth three or four times and required huge amounts of time. A simple ten-page contract might have required five or six hours of an attorney's time, plus a substantial amount of secretarial time in transcribing the document.

Now fast forward to the 1990s. The firm of Dewey, Stikum & Howe has eight partners, fourteen associates, ten secretaries, one accounting clerk, and two legal assistants. Attorneys type their own documents on their computers . They print the drafts themselves on a printer assigned to their station. They make corrections, as appropriate, and alert their secretary. Their secretaries print the final version on bond and, if it is a letter, prepare envelopes.

As can be seen, computerization has permitted the law firm of the nineties to be more efficient in that they can get along with half the secretaries required only twenty years before to perform the same services. In some firms, computerization has allowed firms of modest size to get along with very few secretaries.

Given the fact that superior legal secretaries represent a substantial cost to law firms, this reduction in staffing can have a salutary impact on the profitability of a firm. Computers do not require tax withholding, unemployment compensation, or sick leave. They never need a vacation and rarely complain. The firm can get rid of marginal secretaries, retain the best, and *still* make a substantial cost savings. Are these savings translated into lower fees? Dream on.

While electronic dictation (widely practiced in the 1970s) was inefficient in that it had to be transcribed by a secretary, it was— and remains—generally faster (for the lawyer, at least) than typing drafts. Time/motion studies have demonstrated that attorneys spend less than half the time to produce a draft document by speaking into a Dictaphone than typing it. This is partially a function of lack of typing and computer skills and partially other factors such as interruptability, train of thought, etc.

Thus, while a document can be produced faster if a lawyer types it rather than a secretary, this actually has the effect of increasing bills to clients since the lawyer is billing at his regular hourly rates, while the secretary's costs are still bundled into the hourly rates.

Some traditional lawyers are deathly afraid of the efficiency that computers might theoretically bring to a law firm. For example, some young attorneys are proficient computer operators and can produce drafts, and even finished documents, in less time than it took to write them longhand on a yellow legal pad. (N.B., legal pads are rarely yellow anymore due to the pressure to recycle paper.)

This problem of increased efficiency has been partially solved by the flexibility of computers themselves. While in the Dark Ages, time limits, filing dates, and deadlines required lawyers to be careful in their drafting process and induced them to only go through two or three drafts (since they had to be entirely retyped with each version), today's lawyers think nothing of going through fifteen or twenty drafts on a simple twenty-page document.

It is one of God's miracles that there is a single tree standing in North America given the number of forests denuded by multiple drafts, which lawyers now undertake. This tendency to multiple drafting and correction, of course, expands the time necessary to produce a document, even with the most competent secretaries. (In fact, this book required so many computer-driven revisions that but for the moral rearmament of recycling, the author would be very sad about the number of trees destroyed.)

Law firms also use computers for a wide variety of other tasks in addition to word processing. Most firms use "numbers-crunching" programs for their internal accounting and for client services. Some of these are ubiquitous programs, such as Lotus® or dBase®, others are specialized legal software for maintaining databases, tracking documents in litigation, research, communications, and Desktop Publishing.

Although law firms were relatively late entering the computer age (behind banks, insurance companies, the travel industry, among others), most major law firms today have significant computer capabilities. Although many older lawyers still do not know how to efficiently operate some of their systems, most major firms have Management Information Specialists (a.k.a. techno-nerds) and scrubbed young associates who know the intricacies of software programs and can make them jump through flaming hoops.

As was the case with word processing, however, many of these programs pose a threat to the profitability of firms that have embraced a gross billable hours philosophy. They permit lawyers to accomplish tasks quickly. Form letters can be printed at the touch of a button, court documents (which previously required constant supervision by senior attorneys) now can be prepared on floppy disks by a clerk; internal communications (which used to be done by written memoranda) can now be accomplished by electronic mail. Many of these functions formerly required the use of billable time. Now they can be done cheaply and easily. A disaster.

For some firms, the advent of computers have been a boon. These firms emphasize efficiency over grinding hours. While not yet widespread, firms that do not regard the computer as a threat, but as a tool for serving *clients*, are beginning to make their presence felt in the legal community.

CHAPTER 10

The Cancer of Gross Billable Hours

"There is a growing trend in the legal profession which, left unchecked, threatens the well-being of all lawyers and firms... Some manifestations of these unsound principles...include: compensating lawyers solely on the basis of hours worked rather than on the value or service to clients and contributions to the firm."—"At The Breaking Point" conference report, American Bar Association.

While the gross billable hours standard has made many law firm partners phenomenally wealthy, it contains within it the seeds of its own destruction. Any business that confuses production with productivity is doomed to failure in a free-market economy.

While there is little question that many lawyers work slave-like hours, and partners receive munificent salaries, the value of this work is questionable. As described in prior chapters, law firms produce work in a manner similar to the old Soviet system. People are rewarded not by their efficiency, productivity, or merit, but their ability to generate gross billable hours. Even assuming a lawyer actually works anywhere close to the gross billable hours they indicate on their time sheets, inefficiencies are apparent.

A firm relying on gross billable hours eviscerates itself in a number of other respects.

Any large enterprise requires a number of skills to make it successful. In a law firm, these include expertise, client acquisition, management ability, communications, and a work ethic. The primary use of the gross billable hours standard ignores these factors. It rewards only one thing—the ability to log enormous numbers of hours to a client without reference to how the client was acquired or whether those hours are being used to benefit the client's interests.

Even putting aside the clients' goals, a law firm that rewards *only* the ability of lawyers to spend many hours in the office is sowing the seeds of its own demise. A reward system in a firm that relies upon gross billable hours provides a disincentive for attorneys to serve the interests of the firm and the clients. These include:

Pro Bono. Lawyers in firms that put a premium on gross billable hours are disinclined to provide legal services for anyone other than billable clients. Aside from contingent fee cases, few lawyers (other than the most altruistic) want to work on clients for which they do not get credit. Pro bono clients (those involving issues of general public welfare) wind up at the bottom of the list for attorneys in firms with the gross billable hours bent.

Given the relatively high salaries of lawyers in general, and the low esteem in which the legal profession is held by the public, *more* pro bono work would often serve the public welfare, but gross billable hours firms discourage such activities. This is not to suggest that *pro bono* attorneys are always an unalloyed benefit to the public.

Many pro bono attorneys (those who work *Pro bono publico*— Latin "for the benefit of the public") are sometimes regarded as the heroes of the legal profession. They work without any fees at all. What could be more fair than that? Unfortunately that is sometimes not the case. Pro bono lawyers do *not* work without fees— they are paid (on a salary) which is often very low. While many pro bono attorneys characterize themselves as heroes, often they are a little more than pests in the interest of justice.

Imagining themselves as David in the face of Goliaths and with no incentive to resolve disputes, they clog the legal arteries with motions, appeals, pleadings, and assorted nonsense. Clients may believe they are being done an enormous favor by having a counsel filing reams of paper of their behalf at no cost. This is often not the case. Pro bono attorneys are doing it either for themselves or their benefactors (be it a law firm or foundation which pays them their salary).

If the purpose of a lawyer is to facilitate the resolution of disputes, pro bono lawyers are very often at the opposite end of the spectrum—creating disputes when none need exist. Unshackled by any sort of economics at all, they are free to pursue the most questionable of claims. This is not to suggest that all pro bono attorneys are ill motivated. For certain, many attorneys perform pro bono work as their obligation to the community. This is to be applauded.

Nevertheless, "career" pro bono attorneys should be regarded as suspect at best. They often put their own philosophical goals ahead of the client's immediate interests, preferring to make court cases of issues that could be easily resolved by arbitration or conciliation. The later methods, however, do not guarantee the headlines created by high-profile civil rights, environmental, or criminal cases to which many pro bono attorneys aspire.

If you have a case that will be handled pro bono by *any* attorney, make sure that *your* interest—not those of the attorney or his benefactor—is being served.

Administrative Work. *All* law firms require attorneys to spend some time on firm administration. These duties range from inspecting clients' bills to recruiting new associates. A firm with a premium on gross billable hours necessarily encourages its partners and associates to neglect the efficient operation of the firm.

Professional Education. No matter how well trained an attorney is, he needs continuing legal education. The law is not static; attorneys need to be well versed in the newest developments. There are literally hundreds of seminars and courses available to attorneys to hone their skills. A gross billable hours standard, however, discourages attorneys from improving themselves in that such time is not billable and they are not rewarded for it.

Professional Associations. Most lawyers belong to one or more bar associations and often as many as a half dozen professional associations in their field of specialization. These associations not only provide services to the public but also to the attorneys themselves, providing opportunities for public service, advanced legal education, publishing articles on recent legal developments, and promoting changes in the law.

Lawyers are actively discouraged from participating in these activities, however, if they are a member of a firm with the gross billable hours standard. Since bar association duties are not billable, professional associations suffer from lack of participation by attorneys in their programs.

Overreaching. Many attorneys, especially in larger firms, tend to become specialized in their fields of law. A tax specialist, for example, may never have written a will in her professional career. A communications lawyer may have never litigated a jury trial.

Although most lawyers were taught rudimentary theory of various subjects in law school, one can practice for thirty years and never have occasion to revisit these topics. Large firms generally include lawyers from various disciplines, so attorneys can concentrate in their field of specialization without having to be generalists.

Firms emphasizing gross billable hours, however, defeat the very advantages of their diversity. Many matters, particularly complex financial transactions, require skills in various disciplines. Setting up a company, for example, often involves questions of tax, corporate law, securities, banking, contracts, and other specialties.

In gross billable hours firms, an attorney who is assigned to a new client or a new matter is disinclined to "share hours" with specialists. The more work she *personally* does on the matter, the better she looks. Further, while a specialist may require only three or four hours to resolve a particular problem, an attorney only vaguely familiar with the issues may require a dozen or more hours to come to the same conclusion. This is caused by research time and analysis, which nonspecialists must devote to an issue to bring them up to speed with the specialist's knowledge.

"Hoarding" of hours is common in firms putting a premium on gross billable hours, and attorneys refer matters to specialists only in extreme circumstances.

Not only does this undermine the very advantage a diversified law firm has, but it is unfair to the client. Why should a client pay for twelve hours of Lawyer A's time when the same advice could have been rendered by Lawyer B in two hours? Since there is often not a great deal of difference between the billing rates of various specializations, a client can pay thousands of dollars more for legal advice from a firm that emphasis gross billable hours than one that stresses efficiency.

Economic Cancer. Putting aside all the other things lawyers must forego to achieve gross billable hours, by far the most deadly cancer spawned by this standard is that it promotes the inefficient use of resources.

In most business enterprises in a free-market economy, a premium is put on getting a job done right the first time, in a minimum amount of time, at the lowest possible cost, so as to maximize profitability. These principles are turned on their head in law firms emphasizing gross billable hours. The *least* efficient attorneys are rewarded, while the most efficient are punished.

Many lawyers retort that, "We have nothing to sell but our time." For some lawyers this is undoubtedly true, since they have nothing of value to peddle anyway. Most attorneys, however, *do* have something of value to sell—their professionalism and expertise. When the value of legal skills is debased, the entire concept of professionalism in the law is eroded, and firms are driven to make economic decisions for precisely the wrong reasons. The economics of gross billable hours encourages increasing the number of lawyers in the country since more attorneys can generate more hours. This can be intensely profitable, particularly if many of those lawyers are in the junior ranks.

This principle of leveraging is one of the causes for the high salaries among partners. A merit-based system of both billing and recognizing contributions of attorneys would significantly reduce the number of practicing attorneys in the country to reflect the real demand for services. If lawyers produced more in less time, there would be less need for more lawyers.

Reverse Leveraging. As noted above, the principle of leveraging has traditionally been one of the principles of legal economics. It works like this:

Step 1. Hire a junior associate for $60,000 per year.

Step 2. Multiply the salary by an overhead factor, representing ancillary costs of employing the individual. These include insurance, secretarial assistance, office space, and unemployment compensation taxes. For purposes of illustration, let's use an arbitrary number of 40 percent (although these costs can run anywhere between 30 and 50 percent). $60,000 x 40% = $24,000.

Step 3. Determine the total cost of the associate, by adding salary plus ancillary costs. $60,000 + $24,000 = $84,000.

Step 4. Find enough legal work to do to pay for the associate. Everything else is gravy.

An associate in the above example given sufficient legal work for the firm to bill $100,000, represents a source of profit for the firm of $16,000 a year. This is true no matter what the philosophy of a law firm (i.e., whether it adopts a gross billable hours standard system or not). It is a simple economic fact of life.

In firms that rely exclusively on a gross billable hours standard, however, the above leveraging principle translates into intense pressure to have the associate bill as many hours as possible to achieve the $100,000 goal. In other firms, a $100,000 goal can be achieved on the basis of *merit*. Ironically, the gross billable hours standard system works *against* the profitability of a law firm if the firm also applies the gross billable hours standards to partners.

If partners are *required* to have 1,800 gross billable hours a year, they are likely to do so at the associates' expense. Since partners are responsible for allocating work, they often will keep it to themselves rather than passing it on to an associate. This is destructive to leveraging and profitability of a firm. It is attacks the primary profit center of the firm by transferring work from an associate who needs to cover his cost to a partner.

Demoralization of Attorneys. One of the least quantifiable but most important effects of the gross billable hours system is the declining levels of satisfaction in the profession demonstrated by almost every major study conducted in the last thirty years.

The American Bar Association has noted, "From the lawyers perspective, total dependency from revenues on hours billed means that compensation also is totally dependent on hours billed, which in turn means long hours, burnout, increased family problems and personal stress, and decreased morale."

A recent ABA study on the subject also noted that, "Simply put, if billable hour goals prevent a lawyer from having time for things other than work, that person cannot be a truly good lawyer" without time to pursue whatever outside interests a lawyer has, be it family or a personal hobby, the lawyer 'lives to work' rather than 'works to live.' At a certain point, the demand for billable hours on lawyers become so great that initiatives like better training and communication, or part-time work options that only a handful of lawyers in fact can actually utilize, no long make enough of a difference. At a certain point, lawyers may simply have no life outside the office, with a resulting negative impact on the lawyer, the family, and the firm."

Clients generally want strategic planning, support, counseling, accessibility, and promptness from senior lawyers, but that is not what they get in gross billable hours firms, because senior lawyers are too busy doing low-level work.

Spreading Cancer to Clients. This practice is also unfair to clients. If the work could be done by a less highly paid individual, clients wind up paying partners' hourly rates for work that could have been done at a lower cost.

There is another problem in the gross billable hours system which clearly manifests itself. Firms with such a system of measuring attorneys' competence have every motivation to lengthen legal disputes to the maximum extent possible. Compromise and rapid dispute resolution are anathemas to a gross billable hours firm, even when such results would benefit the client. Lawyers in these firms have a stake in making sure that simple disputes can be elongated to pay for both straightening their children's teeth *and* putting them through Harvard Medical School. It is not unheard of for lawsuits to go on for fifteen or twenty years, without final resolution.

Lawyers are fond of blaming the "clogged court system" for these delays, but it is the lawyers themselves who have clogged the courts. There are few cases that cannot be amicably resolved short of litigation—even when the government is involved.

Even without resort to the Alternative Dispute Resolution panel ("ADR") (discussed below), lawyers can often truncate proceedings by negotiating directly with the other side and striking the best deal. Many are loathe do so, however, because they both enjoy the battle of the courtroom, and to settle disputes without resort to protracted legal proceedings would cut into their pocketbook.

It would be difficult to imagine a situation in any other profession where there is a greater conflict of interest. Clients generally are best served by resolving legal disputes in the shortest period of time at the lowest possible cost. Gross billable hours law firms, necessarily, emphasize the greatest amount of time at the highest possible cost.

Alternative Dispute Resolution. When lawyers are unsuccessful in resolving legal matters in a timely manner, they have rarely taken advantage of Alternative Dispute Resolution unless it is specified in the original contract between the disputing parties. ADR, however, is gaining increasing favor, particularly among commercial enterprises as a way to shorten legal proceedings and reduce overall costs.

Although there are dozens of ADR fora, perhaps the best known in the United States is the American Arbitration Association ("AAA"). In recent years, the AAA reports an increasing use of arbitration rather than litigation by companies. Almost always, arbitration has been specified in the original contracts rather than recommended by counsel after a dispute arises.

The rules of the American Arbitration Association are straightforward. In contrast with court proceedings, AAA arbitrations are a good value for the money. Proceedings are relatively informal, opportunities for procedural tricks and delay are minimal, the outcome is binding on the parties, and both sides to the dispute are generally satisfied with the results—particularly given the fact that they have saved thousands of dollars in legal fees.

The AAA and other alternative dispute resolution procedures ("Rent A Judge," etc.) while still not accounting for a majority of cases, promise clients an opportunity for speedy resolution of their matters at enormous cost savings.

The National Institute of Dispute Resolution (NIDR), a non-profit organization that provides technical assistance and funding for new ADR programs, documents the growth of what its officials prefer to call simply "Dispute Resolution." "We don't see it as 'alternative' anymore," explains Vice-president Thomas A. Fee.

According to NIDR statistics, dispute resolution has become widespread. In 1980, 25 of the nation's 175 law schools offered dispute resolution courses; in 1990, 140 law schools offered them. In 1980 there were just 80 community justice centers to help settle disputes among neighbors, friends, and family members; ten years later there were more than 300. In 1980 there were court-related dispute resolution programs in 17 states; in 1990, all 50 states had them.

Some attorneys will strenuously object to the above analysis on the grounds that a majority of legal disputes are *not* resolved by a final outcome in court but rather by negotiation among the parties, sometimes literally at the courthouse door or before the jury returns with a verdict.

While this is statistically correct, the fact remains that lawyers often stall for years before entering serious negotiations. In part they are motivated by the fact that rapid resolution of a case cuts into their own pocketbook. In fact, pretrial maneuvering (various motions, discovery, etc.) account for more than 90 percent of lawyers' fees in a typical civil case. The trial is simply the "end game" in which a relatively modest proportion of the overall bill is involved. A "motions practice" can go on for years and involve thousands (or even millions) of dollars in legal fees before negotiated settlement is reached. It is in motions practice and discovery where the real fees are generated—not in court.

Recruiting. The gross billable hours syndrome also represents a cancer to the firm's recruiting. Most law firms have summer programs in which law students become "summer associates." That is, they work with the firm for three or four months in the summer and are given assignments to test their legal skills. This system is designed both to allow the students to observe the firm and the firm to observe the students.

Firms compete aggressively to get the best students from the best schools to participate in their summer programs.

In firms that emphasize gross billable hours, however, the system is unfair to the firms, the students, and, ultimately, the clients. Lawyers are disinclined to assign summer associates projects since the work these students do *could* have been done by the lawyer. This necessarily reduces the lawyer's gross billable hours. The summer associate, then, is relegated to doing "make work" projects, which are often contrived and boring. The law firm pays handsome salaries to people who perform little useful work, and the summer associate gets little exposure to the real world of the law.

Clients are often billed for a summer associate's time, but the real danger to clients is the fact that the costs of summer associates are passed on to them in the form of higher hourly fees from the balance of the lawyers in the firm, who must cover the cost of these programs. If the summer associates were allowed to do real work for a client, they might come somewhere close to paying for their costs. In gross billable hours firms, however, this is almost never the case. The summer associates' programs are really designed as a "romancing tool" by law firms for employees, the cost of which is borne by clients.

Corrosion of Ethics. Aside from the public service and economic cancers the gross billable hours system induces, there is an ethical aspect to this disease.

Many attorneys are under intense pressure to bill as many hours as possible and are strongly motivated to maximize their hours by fair means or foul. There are many ways of "cooking the books." Far and away the most common is merely to pad the time sheets. This may be as simple as adding a quarter hour to time it actually took an attorney to accomplish a task or inventing a project for inflating time sheets.

While it is impossible to know with precision how common such practices are, lawyers are rewarded for dissembling on their time sheets and are penalized if they do not in firms that cleave to a gross billable hours standard. This system tempts the most punctilious individual to fudge. The pressure to bill time is so unrelenting, and the penalties for not doing so are so severe, that moral rot is inevitable...and lawyers wonder why they are held in low esteem. The phrase "Honest Lawyer" has entered American folklore as all-too-true oxymoron.

This is not to suggest that all lawyers are perfidious by nature, or even in their general conduct, but merely that the pressures generated by the gross billable hours standard are so intense and pervasive that it is a remarkable individual, indeed (or one who does not work in a gross billable hours firm), who can resist them.

When the public reads about the criminal indictment of a prominent lawyer based upon allegations of systematic cheating or stealing through fraudulent billing practices, the effect has been to eat away at the heart and soul of the profession by corroding the confidence that has traditionally existed between lawyers and clients.

CHAPTER 11

The Solution

Until recently, consumers of legal services have been relatively powerless to attack the system by which legal services are charged. It was difficult to comparison shop among law firms for the best price and highest quality, since most firms refused to provide any guarantees with regard to pricing. About all a client could get was a list of attorneys' hourly rates and a very rough estimate as to how much a project would cost (plus or minus 50 percent). Even here, lawyers routinely overran budgets more often than football coach George Allen did with his Redskins recruiting budget.

A number of remedies were proposed in the late 1970s and early 1980s. Most notable were the standards recommended by the American Corporate Counsel Association (ACCA). The ACCA recommended that its members adopt a standard billing format which law firms should follow. (N.B., The ACCA is composed primarily of "inside" counsel—lawyers who are hired as employees of major companies, both to perform in-house legal services and to select outside counsel.)

The ACCA recommendations were sweeping. Until the late 1970's, it was common for law firms to present five-figure statements to a client with a two sentence explanation of the services rendered.

The ACCA improvements required law firms to provide descriptions of services performed, the attorneys performing them, the amount billed, the amount of time required, and specific breakouts of all expenses. A variation of an ACCA-style bill is included as an illustration in Chapter 12.

During the 1980s, many companies adopted ACCA principles, and today most major law firms prepare bills on some variation of this model. While the ACCA format was unquestionably an improvement, it is not foolproof and may actually work against the interests of the consumers of legal services. No one would suggest that the legal community should revert to the "bad old days" of nondisclosure, but there are some twists to the ACCA system that would improve its utility to the customers and to law firms, as well.

The ACCA format attempts to make law firms' schemes to increase their billings more transparent. Law firms have battled back by relying on the subterfuges described in prior chapters. The ACCA mechanism also presumes that the reviewing party (generally inside counsel in a corporation) is familiar with the operations of a law firm and how long it should take to perform certain projects.

Such reviewing attorneys, however, are rarely intimately involved with day-to-day operations of the firms, and it is virtually impossible to spot some of the contrivances to increase the bill.

The ACCA format is a leap forward but does not solve all problems, particularly for clients lacking the skill, time, and sophistication to critically examine lengthy descriptions of services. This is true even in the largest corporations. Often, companies will hire outside counsel only for areas they cannot handle with their legal staff. By definition, it is difficult for inside counsel to question charges of attorneys working on matters beyond their field of competence.

If the general counsel of a major corporation determines that she needs a specialist in admiralty law for a discrete project, she might not even recognize the terminology in the bill, such as "liabled ship/arrested contents" or "challenged demurrage charge. Even sophisticated companies can be overcharged by law firms with a gross billable hours standard.

The ACCA format has provided a valuable window on law firm bills, but it is far from a total answer to the problem. Much more pervasive surgery is required. What is needed is not a radical approach to the problem but to bring law firms into the twentieth (nineteenth?) century in terms of free-market economics. This is pretty simple stuff. To be successful, law firms should:

- Provide superior service.
- Charge a fair price.
- Make a reasonable profit.

To accomplish these objectives, both for the benefit of the client and the law firm, the solution is good old-fashioned capitalism: agree on the services to be performed, agree on the price to be charged for those services, and let the market take care of the rest.

CHAPTER 12

Fight Back I: Hold the Line on Expenses

Law firms have marvelous ways of unbundling expenses and passing them on directly to clients. There are numerous ways of thwarting this practice. Start with the ACCA recommendations and add several other policies.

Photocopying

1. Establish, in advance, what photocopying charges are to be per page. Some law firms bill double, or even triple, the amount a local retail copying store would charge.

2. Insist that all photocopying charges include a description of each job. Law firms often aggregate photocopying charges for a day, a month, or even a quarter. The client has no way of knowing what was actually copied, how many copies were made, or

103

if their instructions with regard to the per page rate were being followed.

Law firms will object that this will add to their costs. Do not believe them. Almost all law firms now have sophisticated computers attached to their photocopying machines which require each job to be separately billed. The computer printouts of each job can be retrieved. It should only take a photocopying operator a moment or two to mark down a description of the job and how many pages were copied to substantiate the charge.

If a firm still balks at this request, consider another firm. A garage that could not demonstrate it had *really* replaced your oil filter by showing you the old and new filters would be out of business in a hurry if customers discovered that the filter they paid for wound up on another car. Hold the law firm to this. It is simple for them to do; a client deserves it.

Secretarial Overtime. Secretarial overtime is sometimes essential. Outright bans on overtime are unwise. You can, however, limit the conditions under which overtime will be permitted. These include the following.

1. Insist on prior consultation. If an attorney believes that overtime will be required, he should be able to advise you, in advance, explain why the overtime will be required, how much time will be taken, and how much (roughly) it will cost.

2. Be alert to the fact that many law firms, in addition to overtime, also will purchase dinner for their secretaries and cab fare home (or parking)—all of which is passed along to the client. These also can escalate the cost to the consumer of legal services.

3. Be highly critical of an attorney who is not able to get his work done during the workday. This sometimes is a sign of poor time management. An attorney who requests you to grant permission for secretarial overtime at 4:30 in the afternoon may not have been working on your matter during the day and has put it off until the last moment, requiring a secretary to stay over at your expense. In these circumstances, he believes that he holds the club over your head, particularly in instances where very short deadlines are involved. Under these circumstances, it is wise to take a firm position. Tell the attorney that you expect your deadlines to be met, you have no intention of paying overtime, and that it is his responsibility to perform the legal services properly and in an efficient manner. Be difficult about this.

Telephone. Although telephone charges are not generally an area where great abuse exists, you should insist on a breakdown of all toll telephone charges, including who was called, when they were called, and the total charge for the call.

Most attorneys are relatively honest about not making personal calls on clients' accounts, but there are times when this occurs. Since attorneys can pass along all telephone charges to their clients, they are not sensitive to cost savings they might achieve by calling at off-peak hours.

Sometimes telephone calls are obviously unnecessary. This can be revealed by a review of the toll charges which should be reconciled with the time charges. If the hourly charges are not broken down, the law firm should be required to specify, at least, the individual called and the purpose of the call.

Word Processing. Make it clear that you have no intention of paying for word-processing charges, unless specifically authorized in advance. There may be some occasions when word-processing charges are legitimate (putting an entire document into Desktop Publishing Format, typesetting, etc.). These charges should be very rare; word processing should be bundled into the charges of the firm.

If the firm is efficient, they may not even need word processors. If the firm believes it *is* more efficient to use word processing, that is its decision; there is no reason for a client to pay extra for it under most circumstances.

Travel and Entertainment.

1. Apply the same standards to your lawyer as you apply to your business or personal activities. If it is your practice to stay at Motel 6, insist that your attorney does so. If you permit your president, but not your district manager, to stay at the Ritz, develop a standard which is compatible with your company's practice.

Insist on receiving a complete breakdown of travel charges from your lawyer, including where they stayed, where they ate, and any miscellaneous expenses. Law firms may object to this, but they *will* have the records. Most major law firms require attorneys returning from business trips to submit detailed expense accounts which are reimbursed to the lawyers and billed to the client. These can be computer generated. You do not have to necessarily see every receipt, but you should, at least, have access to the expense reports that the lawyer submitted to their firm.

2. Make your policy clear to your attorney before he undertakes any travel on your behalf. Do this in writing. If a dispute arises later, you will be able to demonstrate that you made your policy clear from the start, the law firm accepted it, and that a lawyer violated your policy. The lawyer will have to pay for the overage out of his own pocket and will probably not do it again.

3. Many companies have adopted a per diem standard similar to that of the U.S. government. If you have done so, you don't even need to inquire how or where the attorney spent her money on a trip, so long as she did not exceed a per diem amount.

You should note that per diem costs vary depending upon where you require the attorney to travel. It is much cheaper to visit Tulsa than it is Tokyo. Do not be unreasonable with per diem expenses but insist that they be followed. If an attorney believes that the per diem amounts you think are reasonable are too low, she is free to stay in the Akasaka Prince Hotel in Tokyo, paying the difference between your established per diem and the cost of her ego out of her own pocket.

4. If you have not insisted on a maximum, or negotiated fee, and expect that your matter may involve travel for your attorney, find out her firm's policy with regard to billing you while the attorney is en route. It is not unusual for an attorney to bill a client for the time she spends in the air.

5. Be sure to specify the class of travel for which you will be responsible. Law firms, like most businesses, have policies on whether a lawyer can travel business or even first class. Whatever the firms' policies, they work for you and should conform to *your* policies when traveling on your matters.

Some clients specify that for trips under 1,000 miles, attorneys are expected to fly economy class and purchase their tickets fourteen days in advance, if possible. For trips between 1,000 and 3,000 miles, business class is sometimes authorized, but maximum dollars are specified. First class travel should be rarely authorized, except in extreme circumstances.

6. Some companies have developed complex ceiling amounts that they will pay for travel to various destinations. They, therefore, do not care which class of travel is undertaken by the lawyers, so long as it does not exceed the ceiling. While this has a number of advantages, airline fares change so rapidly, and there are almost infinite number of beginning and ending points, that this is rarely a feasible solution.

7. Many companies with their own travel departments insist that lawyers' travel be booked through them so that not only the class of travel but also the amount can be directly controlled by the client. For larger companies, this is a reasonable solution. Smaller companies can insist that their lawyers be booked through their (the client's) regular travel agent which is familiar with the company's travel policies. In these cases, airline tickets can be picked up at the airport by the attorney or mailed.

8. Specify particular items that you will *not* pay for under any circumstances. Examples of such expenses might include:

♦ In-room movies;

♦ Bar bills, particularly in-room minibars;

♦ Any expense more than $10 unless accompanied by a receipt;

♦ Taxi fares more than $20 when public transportation is reasonably available (to and from airports, for example);

♦ Hotel laundry and dry cleaning costs, unless the trip is more than five days.

...etc.

Insist that hotel bills be submitted with the statements or a full description provided with the statement to assure that these charges are not aggregated with legitimate expenses of an attorney on the road.

Facsimile Transmissions. Facsimiles are fast, but they can be expensive. While the facsimile is often a boon to lawyers and clients alike—especially when communicating across several time zones—it can also be a significant source of overcharging. You can control this by insisting that facsimile charges be computed on a maximum per page amount.

Insist that your bill provide a breakout of how many pages were transmitted, destination, toll charges, and a brief description of the matter. As with copying charges, most law firms have the ability to track every facsimile transmission. Facsimiles are also well suited for transmittal at off-peak hours to achieve substantially reduced telephone charges. Encourage your lawyer to take advantage of such rates. Many facsimile machines can be programmed to transmit documents in the middle of the night, and some do not require individuals to actually run the machine.

Never pay a law firm for receiving a facsimile document. Some law firms (like some hotels) charge upwards of $1 a page to receive facsimiles. This is downright insulting. Refuse to pay such charges.

Messenger Services. Law firms do not hire messengers out of the goodness of their hearts. They hire them because messengers can, and sometimes do, more than pay for themselves. Unbundled messenger fees can run into hundreds of dollars a month.

You should carefully review messenger service charges on your bill and insist that the bill break down the date, name of the messenger (or service), brief description of the document(s), and where it was taken or picked up.

Often, law firms use messengers when the U.S. Post Office would be sufficient. Charges of $8 to $15 are not unusual for a crosstown jaunt. Since private messenger services are highly competitive, it is easy to determine what it should cost to have your documents delivered by calling one of them. If the law firm's charges are significantly out of line with the private messenger services, you should question them.

Develop a Policy—Stick With It. Even small businesses should develop a written policy with regard to expenses they are willing to pay to law firms. This policy should cover at least the items noted in this chapter and should be given to attorneys before they commence work on the company's legal matters.

Sometimes, the firm will protest that your policies are different than those of the firm (that it is the firm's practice to charge $.15 a page for photocopying, and your policy is to pay only $.07 a page). Do not compromise your policies if you believe they are reasonable and realistic. *You* are the customer, they are the provider of services.

If one firm balks at abiding by your policies, there are a dozen others eager to bid for your business. Do not be unreasonable in setting your policies (you should permit some "at cost" recovery of reasonable expenses) but establish a written policy vis-a-vis unbundled fees.

Exhibit A is a sample of written policy a company might give to a law firm that still adopts the gross billable hours philosophy. There are many variations of this policy, but whichever one you select, make sure the law firm abides by it and refuse to pay any bills not conforming with your policy. If, for example, a firm balks at giving you an analysis of hours in tenth-hour segments, find another firm. You are the customer.

Preferably, of course, you won't even need to know how many hours a firm spends on a particular project if you select a firm that has adopted the free-market principles rather than one mired in gross billable hours.

Exhibit B is an example of a policy that a company might adopt with their more enlightened outside counsel.

EXHIBIT A

Counsel Billing Policy [For Gross Billable Hour Firms]

This statement sets forth policy and procedures regarding payment for services rendered by counsel to or on behalf of the Company and/or its subsidiaries.

It is the policy of the COMPANY and its subsidiaries (collectively "COMPANY") that only reasonable charges necessary and appropriate for the accomplishment of the legal services requested will be approved for payment.

Subject always to the above policy, legal statements will be processed for payment when submitted in conformity with the following procedures:

Unless otherwise agreed to in advance and in writing, charges for legal services rendered shall be based solely on standard hourly rates for the partners, associates, and legal assistants performing services. Notification of hourly rates shall be furnished prior to commencement of services, and there shall be advance notification in the event of any increase in such rates.

Counsel will carefully consider the staffing for services to be rendered to COMPANY so as to provide for an appropriate level of services, taking into account the complexity and importance of the matter, as well as the need to avoid surplus staffing and unnecessary expense.

Unless otherwise directed by COMPANY's General Counsel, counsel's statements should cover work done on a monthly basis. Such statements are to be rendered no later than thirty (30) days after the end of the specified billing period.

Counsel's statements shall include:

(a) a brief but descriptive summary of the services performed for each matter handled;

(b) the name of each partner, associate, or legal assistant who worked on each matter;

(c) on a daily basis, the number of hours or fractions thereof spent by each such partner, associate, or legal assistant on each matter denominated in 1/10 hour segments;

(d) the billing rate for each such partner, associate, or legal assistant (this information may be provided in a separate document which can be updated);

(e) expenses and disbursements (separately itemized by category; e.g., the cost of reproduction, long-distance telephone, coach-class air travel, ground transportation, meals, lodging, etc.). Please note that extraordinary items and services supplied by outside vendors must be supported with copies of invoices. The itemization referred to above requires that the statement indicate description of the cost in sufficient degree of detail to allow analysis. For example, photocopying charges should be listed by number of copies, date, and a description of the item copied. It is a policy of the COMPANY not to pay more than $0.8 per copy for photocopying material, unless specifically authorized in writing in advance. Long-distance telephone charges should be specified by date, person called, and a description of the purpose of the telephone call. With regard to travel on the COMPANY's account, it is the policy of the COMPANY not to reimburse counsel for in-room movies, alcoholic beverages, in-room minibar bills of any kind, or entertainment not clearly required by legal services. All travel expenses must be not only summarized on a monthly statement, but receipts from outside vendors (e.g., airlines, restaurants, taxicabs, hotels, etc.) must be submitted with the statement. Photocopies are acceptable;

(f) the total for each matter covered by the billing period;

(g) a separate total for each subsidiary for which work has been performed.

It is the policy of the COMPANY not to pay for overhead expenses such as computer time, overtime expenses, secretarial, clerical, and word processing. The COMPANY will pay for such charges as computer legal research (Lexis®, Westlaw®, etc.) and outside research services if a statement for such activities is given in sufficient detail to permit analysis as to their appropriateness.

COMPANY specifically requests that statements submitted by counsel follow substantially the form attached. Unless otherwise agreed to, only statements that are in accordance with these billing procedures will be processed for payment.

Familiarity with the services performed by counsel is essential to the review and approval of counsel's billings. Accordingly, it is important that the General Counsel be promptly informed of and offered the opportunity to assist in:

(a) development of strategy;

(b) document preparation;

(c) document review;

(d) settlement negotiations, where appropriate; and

(e) conferences with adversary parties, where appropriate.

FORM OF INVOICE (ACCA-style bill)

Attorney	Date	Hours	Description of Services Rendered
DEF	01/02/80	0.4	Review Judge's Order re AB claim; conference w/WXY re ORDER
WXY	01/02/80	0.2	Conference w/DEF re Judge Smith's Order and suing the corporate maker of the note to avoid the possible release of the guarantors.
DEF	01/03/80	0.3	Draft amended complaint.
WXY	01/09/80	0.3	Discussion w/DEF re status and strategy, adding parties.
WXY	01/10/80	0.2	Review complaint prepared by DEF.
DEF	01/16/80	2.7	Prepare for pretrial conference.

Attorney	Date	Hours	Description of Services Rendered
DEF	01/17/80	4.1	Prepare for hearing; research re release of guarantors; court appearance; conference with WXY; prepare order.
MS	01/17/80	2.0	Preparation of documents at DEF's instruction.
WXY	01/18/80	1.7	Meeting w/Judge Smith; memorandum to client re status.
DEF	01/22/80	0.2	Review and revise memorandum
WXY	01/30/80	0.1	Conference w/client re settlement.

TOTAL HOURS 12.2   TOTAL FEES $2,108.50

Date	Disbursement	Description
01/19/80	$1.20	Copying expenses @...cent/page

Summary by Attorney	Classification	Hours	Rate/Hour	Totals
W. X. Young	Partner	2.5	250.00	625.00
D. E. Faircloth	Associate	7.7	175.00	1,347.50
M. N. Summers	Legal Assistant	2.0	68.00	136.00

TOTAL FEES. 2,108.50

TOTAL DISBURSEMENT CHARGES. 1.20

TOTAL THIS STATEMENT 2,109.70

As noted previously, it is a far better policy for the Company to force—or at least encourage—its outside counsel to abandon gross billable hours and adopt free-market principles of providing legal services. Even here, however, the client should have a written policy. Exhibit B is an example of counsel billing policy when dealing with free-market firms. It is much more liberal in some respects than Exhibit A. This is because the burden of efficiency is placed on the law firm itself rather than on the client.

EXHIBIT B

Counsel Billing Policy [For Free-Market Firm]

This statement sets forth policy and procedures regarding payment for services rendered by counsel to, or on behalf of, the Company and/or its subsidiaries.

It is the policy of the Company and its subsidiaries (collectively "COMPANY") that legal services be provided to it on the basis negotiated in advance with outside counsel. A description of the legal services to be provided by counsel and the price thereof, is listed in Attachment A hereto. COMPANY notes that it will not be liable for charges in excess of those listed in Attachment A and consistent with the policies noted below in the absence of an explicit written agreement between COMPANY and counsel.

Counsel may submit monthly statements for its fees not to exceed ___% of the total fee listed in Attachment A, together with expenses incurred in the prior month. Counsel's statement should include a brief summary of the services performed. Expenses and disbursements should be separately itemized by categories consistent with the policy noted below.

It is the policy of the COMPANY not to pay for overhead expenses such as computer time, overtime expenses, secretarial, clerical, and word processing. The COMPANY will pay for such charges as computer legal research (Lexis®, Westlaw®, etc.) and outside research services if a statement for such activities is given in sufficient detail to permit analysis as to their appropriateness.

Familiarity with the services performed by counsel is essential to the review and approval of counsel's billings. Accordingly, it is important that the General Counsel be promptly informed of the opportunity to assist in (a) development of strategy; (b) document preparation; (c) document review; (d) settlement negotiations (where appropriate); and (e) conferences with adversaries parties (where appropriate).

Expenses and disbursements (separately item-ized by category; e.g., the cost of reproduction, long-distance telephone, coach-class air travel, ground transportation, meals, lodging, etc.). Please note that extraordinary items and services supplied by outside vendors must be supported with copies of invoices. The itemization referred to above requires that the statement indicate description of the cost in sufficient degree of detail to allow analysis. For example, photocopying charges should be listed by number of copies, date, and a description of the item *copied. It is a policy of the COMPANY not to pay more than $0.8 per copy for photocopying material, unless specifically authorized in writing in advance. Long-distance telephone charges should be specified by date, person called, and a description of the purpose of the telephone call. With regard to travel on the COMPANY's account, it is the policy of the COMPANY not to reimburse counsel for in-room movies, alcoholic beverages, in-room minibar bills of any kind, or entertainment not clearly required by legal services. All travel expenses must be not only summarized on a monthly statement, but receipts from outside vendors (e.g., airlines, restaurants, taxicabs, hotels, etc.) must be submitted with the statement. Photocopies are acceptable.*

ATTACHMENT A

Description of Legal Services

The COMPANY desires to retain the services of Moon, Starz & Sunz (Counsel) to perform legal services as follows:

1. Establish a trading company in Florida with a subsidiary in the Cayman Islands. These companies shall be nominally capitalized and have only one class of shares. All shares should be held by the COMPANY;

2. Provide opinion letters and other legal advice with regard to the tax status of these companies vis-a-vis U.S. and Cayman tax laws;

3. Affect all appropriate registrations and jurisdictions where this is required;

4. Secure trademark registration for the COMPANY's products in the Cayman Islands;

5. Provide documents (e.g., certified copies of Articles of Incorporation, etc.) sufficient to enable the COMPANY to do business in the above-cited jurisdictions;

6. It is understood by the COMPANY that counsel may need to secure the services of advisors in the Cayman Islands. This is specifically authorized by this Agreement, provided that such outside assis-

tance does not cost more than $5,000. It is also understood that the following costs will be borne by the COMPANY: registration fees, notary fees, and such other fees as may be lawfully charged by the jurisdictions named above;

7. For these services the COMPANY agrees to pay counsel the sum of $12,000 to be divided in three monthly payments commencing on June 1, 1995;

8. Counsel undertakes and commits to complete these tasks no later than September 1, 1995.

The above stipulations are subject to the general policies of the COMPANY to which this attachment is appended.

"Lawyers are like beavers: They get in the mainstream and dam it up."

John Naisbitt

CHAPTER 13

Fight Back II: Reward Efficiency

"Clients simply will not pay law firms any more money. Indeed, they already want to pay less and will end up doing so through increased competition for many types of legal services. If lawyers do not take the lead, and develop innovative styles of billing, clients will start dictating fees and will start getting proposals on the same matter from different firms."—"At the Breaking Point" conference report, American Bar Association, 1991.

As noted throughout this book, most major law firms have adopted a policy of billing their clients on an hourly basis and rewarding partners and associates according to the number of hours they can generate. This encourages law firms to act in the most inefficient way possible, which translates into higher incomes for the lawyers, and stratospheric fees for the clients.

To break this cycle of inefficiency and inflation, clients must take a stand. The first step is for clients to directly attack the cause of inefficiency and overbilling by encouraging law firms to abandon the gross billable hours philosophy. This is a five-step process.

Step 1. Find out if your law firm uses gross billable hours as a measure by which it compensates its attorneys. Law firms are reluctant to discuss internal matters. Some will go so far as to tell a client it's none of their business how a firm pays its lawyers. Wrong. It is *you* who is compensating the lawyers, and you have every right to know whether the law firm has adopted policies that guarantee inefficiency and huge legal bills.

Step 2. Express your strong disapproval of the gross billable hours system. Tell the managing partner of the firm that you are willing to pay a fair price for legal services but do not want to have your (unsupervised) vendors of those services motivated more by the desire to chalk up huge hours on their time sheets than by delivering legal services.

Also explain to the managing partner that your company has budgets (he may never have heard of a budget). Buying legal services, like purchasing other goods or services, has to fit within a financial plan. By definition, the "open-ended" costs characteristic of firms with a gross billable hours standard are difficult to reconcile with the concept of fiscal responsibility.

Step 3. Negotiate. For many years, law firms dealt with their clients on a "take-it-or-leave-it" basis. If they marketed themselves at all, it was on the basis of their range of expertise and office locations. It was rare for a firm to actually compete on the basis of price.

In major metropolitan areas, larger law firms are similar in their range of "products." While some have greater expertise than others in particular areas of law, all have similar capabilities in terms of computer backup support, and staff. Because of this, you should chose the most price-competitive and responsive lawyers.

You, the client, should abandon the assumption that setting legal fees is totally within the discretion of the law firm. *You* are paying the bill, and *you* have the right to negotiate on any basis you choose. Establish this prerogative before your retain the services of the firm.

Step 4. Insist on fixed prices. Once you have established the principle of your right to negotiate, insist that

♦ The law firm agrees to abide by your guidelines for expenses;

♦ They provide you a detailed written description of the services they intend to perform on your behalf;

♦ They give a price estimate (within 10 percent);

♦ They estimate the time in days, weeks, or months necessary to accomplish the services and provide a deadline for completion.

It is at this stage that law firms will dig in their heels. They will insist they simply cannot estimate how much time something will take.

Do not accept this as an answer. If the firm is as good as they purport to be, they should be able to come up with an estimate and stick to it. If they do not know how to do this, find another law firm.

Step 5. Tell the law firm that you appreciate their offer but make it clear that you are going to seek competitive bids on your project. Do not make your selection on the basis of price alone. There are numerous intangibles in the selection of a law firm, including your personal relationship with them, their expertise, punctuality, and other factors.

Nevertheless, law firms have been able to get away with economic murder for years by having open-ended bills. You can at least put a stop to that. Follow these same procedures with at least three other law firms before you decide on the firm to handle your matters.

Other ways to reward a law firm's efficiency include the following:

◆ Insist on an arbitration clause in most contracts. Alternative Dispute Resolution procedures are much less expensive for the client than open-ended litigation clauses. They can also lead to the resolution of disputes in a shorter period of time. Because of this, gross billable hours firms find them distasteful. If you are faced with a legal dispute arising under an agreement that contains an arbitration clause, you should consider retaining counsel on the basis of partial contingency rather than billable hours. This is much more of a "roll of the die" proposition for a law firm, but free-market firms often jump at the chance to demonstrate their efficient use of time and arbitral skills. Also consider giving bonuses for success of legal matters. Variable bonuses can encourage counsel to act in the most efficient manner possible, both for your benefit and their own.

◆ Wherever possible, build in a "bonus" for rapid completion of tasks and penalties for delays. Although this policy carries risks of slipshod legal work, generally you want to reward getting the job done efficiently and quickly rather than encouraging lawyers to drag simple matters out to their maximum extent. A "cap" on fees has the effect of a penalty for delay and should be seriously considered. You should note that in certain proceedings, particularly with government agencies, delays are inherent in the system and are beyond any lawyer's control. Licensing matters, for example, can be tedious, particularly if a matter has to go through several layers of government bureaucracy. Here fixed fees may be more appropriate than bonuses for speed.

◆ Be sure to cooperate with your lawyer at every step of any legal proceeding. One of the greatest causes of delay and increased legal fees is clients failing to provide counsel with full and complete data in a timely manner. Lawyers implicitly charge extra for finding out the "true facts." Every lawyer would agree with the statement, "I have never had a client who told me all the facts the first time." This proclivity of clients to put the best face on their legal proceeding in initial conversations with counsel is expensive. Lawyers charge more for finding and correcting the facts later. Be aggressive in providing the facts to your counsel—but insist that they reciprocate by giving you timely and affordable legal services.

Legal Fee Consultants

In recent years, a new breed of mammal has been spawned: the so-called "legal fee consultant." These consultant firms claim to be able to reduce your legal expenses by huge amounts, merely by reviewing the statements you have received from your law firm.

In some cases, these claims may be partially accurate; the means by which they achieve this conclusion are questionable at best. Often, the legal fee consultant is an attorney herself but possesses no particular expertise in the area of law in question. How, for example, could a specialist in real estate even *begin* to analyze a legal bill relating to litigation involving international secured debentures?

Many legal fee consultants assume that the billing law firm has attempted to rip off the client by charging excessive fees. This is not always the case. Sometimes the fees are not only reasonable but a bargain—but the legal fee consultant does not get *paid* unless *some* overcharging is found. Further, since they are paid on a contingency basis, legal fee consultants often question perfectly legitimate charges.

You should be as wary of this means of reducing legal fees as you are of law firm charges *themselves*. As a client, you should remember that a lawyer is there to help *you* solve your own problems—not to solve them herself. *You* (perhaps with the help of this book) are in the best position to judge whether your lawyer's charges are reasonable.

Obviously, law firms routinely overcharge their clients, but it does not take a so-called "consultant" who is motivated by his *own* greed to get excessive charges lowered. In almost all cases, you should save the contingent fee charged by consultants who are less familiar with your matters than you are. Do it yourself. It does not take a consultant to tell you that you should not be paying for your lawyer's breakfast doughnut.

BOOK II

How Law Firms CAN PROSPER

by Joining the Market Economy

CHAPTER 14

Gross Billable Hours: The Alternative

> *"To improve financial performance, most firms have focused on the billable hour. Unquestionably, it has become the primary (at some firms the only) gauge of success, basis of reward, and source of self-esteem. The times have changed, and with change has come a growing need for partners to refocus their attention..."*—Rebecca M. Morrow, editor *Partners Report*, Institute of Management and Administration

Book I concentrated on the unfairness of the gross billable hours system to clients. Of equal importance is the fact that emphasis on gross billable hours by a law firm erodes its ability to be competitive and to maximize its profitability. Firms that put a premium on gross billable hours ignore the most important factor in a free-market enterprise—net income—since there is little incentive to control costs or to work efficiently. Such firms merely rely upon massive amounts of cash to generate profits.

Law firms that abandon the gross billable hours method, however, need not forego handsome profits. All it takes is a businesslike attitude and an emphasis on those factors that make any business in a free market successful: cost containment and efficiency. Superior service to clients can still be achieved with lower gross bills and higher profits to the firm. In this sense, everyone wins. How can this be done? Here are the basic considerations:

♦ Acknowledge the futility of the gross billable hours system, and make a *public* break with it. This includes not only announcing to your clients that you will henceforth be billing on a negotiated price basis but that your attorneys will be rewarded for their efficiency in serving clients within budgets.

Some firms which have selected this route have gone so far as to abolish time sheets entirely; others have retained them as an internal management tool to determine how long it takes various people to accomplish specific goals. In either case, attorneys are rewarded for how *little* time it takes to accomplish a project—not how much.

Your public commitment to this change is essential to discourage backsliding. Dozens of firms have adopted this course in the last two years and have generally found that a public commitment to efficiency and the free market is critical for the success of the program.

In one of the most revealing studies in the past decade, the ABA concluded in 1991 that the most important problem facing the practice of law today was unsound management practices, the most important of which was, "encouraging lawyers to sacrifice, rather than dedicate themselves to their firm by working ever-increasing billable hours."

Your public acknowledgment of this truth is as important to changing your way of doing business as passing through the "denial stage" is for a recovering alcoholic. The firm's credibility must be on the line here. Lip service is not enough.

◆ Develop policies to implement your free-market program in writing. Discuss these policies with attorneys and staff to make certain they are clearly understood and that this represents a clear break with the gross billable hours mentality. Your policy should contain understandable guidelines for attorneys in terms of their promotion and compensation. Although some firms continue to have subjective methods of compensating partners, even after adopting a free-market philosophy, this generally leads to dissension. While it is certainly true that many intangibles go into compensation decisions, some objective guidelines should be provided.

Whichever system is adopted, however, it should have a reasonable degree of predictability, so partners will know that if they adopt efficient work habits, they will be rewarded accordingly. In these calculations, gross billable hours should be irrelevant.

Since the partners are to be compensated on the basis of net fees received, it makes little difference whether they spent one hour or ten hours on the project—except to themselves.

Assume the firm receives $1,000 for two equivalent projects: Partner A worked on her matter for two hours, Partner B worked on his matter for six hours. Under a free-market compensation scheme, both would receive the same amount.

Partners are free to choose their own lifestyles. Some will want to maximize income by taking on additional work, others will be satisfied with their current income and more time off. Either way, partners are rewarded for their efficiency, not the amount of hours they were able to log on their time sheets.

♦ Institute tough cost-control methods. Some firms believe that by merely cutting out free sodas for the staff, or holding their firm Christmas party at McDonald's instead of the Plaza, they can achieve real cost control. This is hokum. Such Draconian measures often do more to hurt morale than they do to boost the net revenues of the firm.

Firms that adopt gross billable hours formulas generally try to unbundle as many costs as possible, and there is very little motivation to be cost conscious.

A free-market law firm has every motivation to be efficient but not parsimonious. Make it clear to your clients that most costs will be bundled and that you will be responsible for their containment. Be specific about which costs are legitimately passed on (long distance telephone calls, out-of-town travel, etc.), but be equally clear on costs which are *not* to be passed on to clients.

A principle often forgotten by law firms is that it rarely pays to rip off your best clients. Many larger firms are discovering this.

In rejecting outlandish charges to clients for photocopying, fax machines, etc., the managing partner of Kirkland & Ellis (one of Chicago's largest firms) noted, "We have rejected the concept of law firm profit centers based on ancillary, clerical, and support services sold to clients." It immediately marked down its charges for such services by up to 50 percent.

While this action undoubtedly cost Kirkland & Ellis some short-term profits, the long-term goodwill it generated will more than offset these immediate costs. Further, an action such as that taken by Kirkland & Ellis (and others) can only help to restore some of the confidence in the integrity of lawyers which has been badly blemished by the greedy "profit machines" present in many gross billable hours firms. These firms have to make up for the inefficiency inherent in their philosophy by overcharging for ancillary services.

No doubt, a firm such as Kirkland & Ellis will discover numerous areas for increased efficiency to more than offset short-term losses occasioned by their principled action.

◆ Link compensation *both* to the firm overhead and income. The greatest inducement for partners to pay attention to costs is if such costs directly affect their personal income. Firms should make cost control a vital element of compensation. Most firms today spread costs more or less evenly among the entire partnership. This system creates no inducement for an individual partner to curtail excessive use of firm overhead, particularly personnel resources. Firm policies with regard to cost control can go only so far without breeding resentment among partners since it is "externally" imposed. If a partner has *personal* inducement to controlling costs, however, these measures can be much more effective.

CHAPTER 15

Controlling Costs

"Ultimately, technology should save the firm and clients money. Hereto, however, the opposite frequently has happened. Fax machines, computers, and other forms of technology are very expensive. Too often, decisions are made to purchase them as though they were toys. New machines are bought, even though existing ones are perfectly serviceable, and the new ones offer only minor advantages. Also, technology has become a status symbol, resulting in decisions to purchase being based on factors other than need. These technology costs go straight to the bottom line, increasing overhead pressures on the firm, and thus pressures on lawyers to bill more."—"At the Breaking Point", American Bar Association 1991.

In the 1960s and 1970s, the rule of thumb was that profits (i.e., distributions to partners) should equal approximately 50 percent of costs. The adoption of gross billable hours as a standard in the industry radically changed those ratios. Today, it is not unusual in large law firms for expenses to be 70 percent of gross income.

There are hundreds of examples of cost containment that have never even occurred to law firms embracing the gross billable hours standard. A few of these include:

◆ Computer training. Although most law firms have computers, the ability of many lawyers to use them efficiency is questionable. Insist that all personnel—including lawyers—be adequately trained on your computer systems. Many firms have found that with adequately trained lawyers, they need less support staff.

This is particularly true for legal research. With some on-line services charging up to $300 an hour, it is essential that lawyers be able to find what they are looking for in a minimum amount of time. Make sure that before anyone is allowed to do on-line computer research, they have been trained and *tested* to be sure they are competent.

◆ Cost Audits. Institute a program of thorough cost auditing. Many law firms lump overhead costs into basket categories, such as "supplies" and "rent and utilities." Broad descriptions such as these may be fine for an annual financial report but are of little help in determining specifically where costs are too high.

Break down your expenses to the greatest extent possible, for the shortest period feasible (monthly is best). Use your computers to assist you. There are dozens of off-the-shelf software programs specifically designed for inventory and cost control that can be run on PCs. A generic item, such as "supplies," for example, might be broken down as follows:

Supplies
Copy paper
Letterhead
Envelopes
   (1) Letter
   (2) 8 ½" x 11"
   (3) Legal
Tape
Paper clips
Highlighters
Pens
Pencils
Magnetic tape
Batteries
Dictaphones
Computer disks
Business cards

Although this might appear to be a great deal of work, consistent attention to these details can reveal surprises. After you have loaded this information into your computer, review it on a monthly basis for costs per item, then request bids for these items from various vendors.

One firm was astonished to discover that the vendor with which it had been buying photocopy paper for more than twenty years was charging 100 percent more than was available from a competitor down the street. By changing vendors, it was able to save $20,000 a year on this item alone. You purchase these items in any event, so keeping a record of what you buy and what it costs is not only prudent but essential for an efficient law firm.

 ◆ Regularly review your personnel needs. Although lawyers are fond of complaining that they don't have enough staff, often the problem is that they don't know how to use existing staff efficiently. Since personnel costs are generally the largest overhead item of a law firm, it deserves the most scrutiny. This is not to suggest that a free-market law firm should be chintzy with salaries or benefits. Many free-market firms have found they can increase efficiency by hiring the best people, pay them well, and get along with fewer of them.

If all attorneys in the firm are competent in word processing, and you have a well-developed policy with regard to the use of word-processing facilities, lawyers should be able to type most of their own drafts, relieving secretaries from this task. Some firms have found they can entirely abolish word-processing centers if they have a well-coordinated local area network (LAN) among attorneys and secretaries.

By encouraging efficient work habits among all personnel (such as using electronic mail rather than typing; printing, copying, and distributing internal memoranda; relying on voicemail rather than receptionists; hiring part-time secretarial help in crunch periods rather than full-time employees) law firms can cut their personnel costs dramatically while actually increasing the compensation and morale of the remaining staff.

Be generous with dollars, but pinch the pennies. Contrary to popular wisdom, a penny pinched is a dollar saved. Walk through any major law firm today, and you will see dozens of examples of waste which could be either turned to profit or towards increasing the morale productivity and general professionalism of the firm. The following are a few examples.

◆ Recycling. While many law firms recycle used paper, often they recycle it too soon. Drafts can be done on the backside of documents, effectively doubling the lifetime of a ream of paper. You can avoid confusion on drafts by inserting the date and number of the drafts on the bottom of the page (most word-processing programs permit this to be done automatically). Notepads and buck slips can also be made from recycled paper. Such notepads can be made a nominal cost in-house and can save a substantial amount in outside printing costs, as well as the cost of the paper.

◆ Centralize your supply room. "Leakage" of office supplies is a major cost for many law firms. Petty pilferage of pens, paper, batteries, floppy disks, and other such items can run into thousands of dollars each year. Establish a central supply room. Assign a person to run it (who can also perform other tasks, such as operating photocopy machines and postage meters), and make sure that all staff—partners and clerks alike—must go there to get supplies.

This need not require elaborate procedures. Requisition forms only add costs. The main purpose of a central supply room is to reduce the inducement to the staff and attorneys to merely wander through the supply room, grab a handful of pencils and highlighters, and put them in their briefcases. Truly larcenous individuals will be able to beat this system, but it does reduce petty theft.

♦ Establish an Internal Recruitment Center. Headhunters are expensive. When you need to replace staff, some of your best prospects are friends of your existing staff. Pay a finder's fee to your staff if they successfully refer someone to your office. This saves, not only the headhunter's fee but advertising costs, agency fees, and interviewing time. It also provides another method for your staff to build community spirit.

♦ Establish a reward fund, particularly for staff suggestions on ways in which the firm could save money. Pass a portion of the savings along to the staff member who made the suggestion. You will find for every ten suggestions you receive, one will be cost effective. Nevertheless, some firms have been able to save substantial amounts of money from staff recommendations. Remember, they deal with the minutiae of the firm every day and are often in a better position to see causes of waste than the most senior partner.

Hold the Line on Associates' Salaries

Over the past decade, the starting salary for associates right out of law school has far outpaced the rate of inflation. It is not unusual today for a twenty-seven-year-old graduate of a major law school to command a $70,000 salary the first year on the job. Under most circumstances, it is difficult for a firm a recoup this amount.

Firms with the gross billable hours standard attempt to do so by making first-year associates log unbelievable time. They know, however, that a substantial amount of that time will have to be written off due to the inexperience of the associate. Many law firms regard the first two or three years of an associate's practice as little more than an apprenticeship where they are given tedious tasks to familiarize themselves with specific areas of law. These assignments sometimes can be done by more experienced legal assistants at lower rates.

The salaries paid to new associates is due, in large measure, to the ferocious competition among larger firms for the graduates who ranked in the upper 3 percent of their class in Ivy League law schools. Bidding wars are common in such legal centers as Boston, New York, Philadelphia, Washington, Chicago, Atlanta, Houston, San Francisco, and Los Angeles. Although the competition is keen, it spills over into all recruiting practices.

It is common for all members of an entering class of a large law firm to be paid the same starting salaries. Firms judge themselves against each other in relation to the proportion of new associates who were editors of law reviews while they were still in law school. However, it is highly questionable whether serving as an editor of a law review is a good indication that an individual will be a superior lawyer. What is clear is that the base rate competition among law firms has driven associates' salaries far beyond any reasonable measure of their immediate worth to a firm.

Many law firms argue that this is not altogether bad in that they have an investment in their associates that they expect to recoup in later years. It does, however, put enormous pressure on the cost side of managing a firm when hundreds of thousands of dollars are being paid to people who cannot cover those costs.

Since associates are employees of a firm, their salary is only the starting point in determining how much they actually cost. For example, if an associate is paid $70,000, a good rule of thumb is to add another 50 percent to that to determine total costs to the firm (including Social Security taxes, insurance, overhead.)

While some costs are unavoidable, it is possible to attract legal talent while at the same time reducing costs. The free market provides the answer. Many firms are turning away from stratospheric base salaries for beginning associates and establishing more realistic foundations. One major law firm broke ranks with its competitors in 1992 by lowering its entering base salary by $5,000 and adopting a merit bonus system, which permits associates to earn substantially more than their competitor's base.

This is a good start but doesn't go far enough. In many firms, bonuses are granted not for efficiency but on the basis of gross billable hours. This system encourages associates to work as inefficiently as possible and rewards precisely the wrong sort of activity. Merit bonuses, however, can be extremely valuable both to the law firm and to the associate, if they are linked to speed, accuracy, client relations, and professionalism.

To achieve these goals, base salaries should be set as low as possible consistent with competitive circumstances, but merit bonuses should be generous and permit the associate to surpass his peers who joined gross billable hour firms.

This approach, however, requires thorough preparation. The standards for receiving merit bonuses must be clear, objective, and *written*. It is also important that a firm not prejudice an associate's chance of getting a merit bonus by assigning her to matters under which she cannot fulfill the criteria. While starting associates are, of course, expected to do whatever work is necessary, firms should find out where a beginning associate has the greatest expertise and interest and allow them to develop their legal skills in areas where efficiency is likely to increase most rapidly.

Since associates do not have the same degree of control over which clients they work for as do partners, and generally find it more difficult to attract business, merit pay systems for associates must be different than the compensation system outlined for partners. Nevertheless, the same types of skills should be rewarded—efficiency, professionalism, and cost savings. While diligence certainly should be one of the factors to be considered, this should not ordinarily be judged by mere reference to the gross billable hours an associate was able to log on his time sheets. Associates should be reviewed at least quarterly using a standard format which is explained to them in advance.

Exhibit C is an example of such a format.

EXHIBIT C

Attorney Evaluation Worksheet—Annual
(Evaluation Period =   )

Contact During Evaluation Period _____

Attorney _____**Class** _____

Evaluator _____**Date** _____

Key: 0   Unsatisfactory
1   Needs Improvement
2   Meets Expectations
3   Exceeds Expectations
4   Truly Exceptional

GENERAL ATTRIBUTES	0	1	2	3	4
1. ANALYSIS/PROBLEM SOLVING					
2. JUDGMENT					
3. DECISIVENESS/DECISION MAKING					
4. CREATIVITY/IMAGINATION					
5. PRODUCTIVITY					
6. EFFICIENCY					
7. FLEXIBILITY					
8. THOROUGHNESS/ATTENTION TO DETAIL					
9. INTERPERSONAL SKILLS					
10. TIMELINESS					
11. JOB COMMITMENT: Effort/Willing to Stretch					

PROFESSIONALISM	0	1	2	3	4
12. RESEARCH SKILL					
13. KNOWLEDGE OF THE LAW					
14. WRITING: CLEAR/CONCISE/EFFECTIVE					
15. ORAL EXPRESSION: COGENT/EFFICIENT					
16. ADVOCACY/REPRESENTATION OF CLIENT					
17. MEETS CLIENTS' NEEDS					
18. MANAGES WORKLOAD					
19. JOB COMPLETION/FOLLOW-THROUGH					
PROFESSIONALISM / CLIENT RELATIONS	**0**	**1**	**2**	**3**	**4**
20. SELF-MOTIVATION/INITIATIVE					
21. PROFESSIONAL DEVELOPMENT (FIRM, CEB, BAR)					
22. PRO BONO ACTIVITIES					
23. OTHER CONTRIBUTION TO COMMUNITY					
24. CONTRIBUTION TO FIRM: Non Client Matters					
25. ABILITY TO RETAIN CLIENTS					
26. ABILITY TO ATTRACT BUSINESS					
27. BUSINESS DEVELOPMENT ACTIVITIES					
OVERALL EVALUATION	**0**	**1**	**2**	**3**	**4**
28. FOR EVALUATION PERIOD					
29. FOR CAREER TO DATE					

A. DESCRIBE THE PRINCIPAL STRENGTHS OF THIS ATTORNEY. GIVE SPECIFIC EXAMPLES. _____

_____

_____

_____

_____

B. DESCRIBE AREAS IN WHICH THIS ATTORNEY'S WORK COULD HAVE BEEN IMPROVED. GIVE SPECIFIC EXAMPLES. _____

_____

_____

_____

_____

C. EVALUATE THIS ATTORNEY'S PROFESSIONAL COMPETENCE, COMMENTING ON HER OR HIS "GENERAL ATTRIBUTES," "PROFESSIONAL SKILLS." AND "PROFESSIONALISM" EVALUATED ON THE PREVIOUS PAGES. EXPLAIN *EACH* ITEM MARKED "TRULY EXCEPTIONAL" OR "UNSATISFACTORY." IF YOUR COMMENTS RELATE TO ANY TIME OTHER THAN THE CURRENT EVALUATION PERIOD, PLEASE SO SPECIFY. _____

_____

_____

_____

_____

_____

_____

In addition to encouraging the type of professional qualities desirable in a lawyer, abandonment of reliance on a strictly gross billable hours standard of reward for associates can have other, intangible benefits.

According to Dr. Edward A. Dreyfuss, a clinical psychologist in private practice in Santa Monica, California, "Many firms no longer view the associate as someone to be trained under the tutelage of a seasoned attorney. Rather, associates are viewed as independent servants who are expected to earn their keep as soon as possible with as little help from the partners as possible. They are considered a source of relatively cheap labor who can be worked seven days a week, twelve hours or more a day and make a profit for the firm doing all the things the partner does not want to do." Firms have developed reputations for how much they paid associates—not how well they trained associates. Because of this state of affairs, associates have begun looking at the job market as a place where the highest bidder wins. They view themselves as commodities in a fair-trade economy. The laws of supply and demand prevail.

Such firms have developed an "eat-'em-up-and-spit-'em-out" image among associates. Associates report that these firms do not expect an associate to have a life outside the firm, or at best, whatever life they may have should be subordinated at the profitability of the firm.

In firms stressing professionalism, however, it is to the firm's and the associate's advantage to emphasize efficiency, sharing of work, and training. Regular meetings between partners and associates, focusing on the needs of associates and listening to their concerns, observations and ideas, are profitable.

Dr. Dreyfuss concludes, "If a firm views associates solely as a source of revenue, they will view the firm as merely a paycheck. No loyalty will develop. Associates should be encouraged to develop outside interests, family ties, and pro bono activities. By investing in developing a well-rounded attorney, the firm will benefit in the long run with more productive, committed, loyal, creative lawyers; this will be reflected in the bottom line."

CHAPTER 16

Down with Gross Billables;
Up with Net Receipts

Partners, in particular, should be rewarded for client acquisition, supervision of associates, working on client matters, public service, and other factors. It is critical, however, that compensation be based upon *net* fees received rather than on gross hours billed. Partners should not be rewarded until the money comes in the door.

It would be inconceivable for any business to pay its owners on the basis of unprofitable work, and profit can generally only be measured when the check clears the bank.

This is particularly true in recessionary times. In the past few years, the net receivables for most major law firms have increased substantially as clients have tightened their belts. Firms' "inventories" of accounts receivable have burgeoned, and write-offs (both of work in process and accounts receivable) have markedly increased. Further, the likelihood of collecting accounts receivable as they age goes down. The Institute of Management and Administration's *Partners Report*, notes the following:

Time Outstanding (No. of Days)	Likelihood of Collectability (By Period Outstanding)
0 — 30	95%
31 — 60	90%
61 — 90	85%
91 — 180	65%
181 — 365	50%
More than 365	40%

In a gross billable hours firm, a partner is paid for the hours he worked, not the amount that was actually collected for that work. Further, there is little incentive for partners to aggressively attempt to collect for work done if they are rewarded whether the money is ever collected or not. There should be a built-in incentive for partners to collect outstanding receivables. This can be best achieved by linking partners' compensation and advancement to *collections* rather than gross billable hours.

How does one get from gross billable hours to net receipts? This relatively straightforward question has confounded some of the best legal minds in the country. Let's start with definitions.

Gross billable hours. Hours marked on time sheets by timekeepers (whether attorneys or legal assistants).

Work in Process (WIP). Gross billable time logged but not yet billed or otherwise acted upon. Generally, law firms bill (at most) once a month, and the gross billable hours logged between one billing cycle and the next are regarded as "Work in Process." It should be noted, however, that if hours are not billed during a billing cycle, they continue as "Work in Process" until they are actually billed.

Accounts Receivable. Amounts billed but not yet paid by the client.

From these definitions, it is easy to see how significant attrition can result from a gross billable hours standard. Assume, for example, that an attorney marks down 100 hours for a client matter on her time sheets. On a gross billable hours basis, it might appear that the work she has done that month is "worth" $25,000 (100 hrs. x $250/hr.). This is almost *never* the case.

At the end of the billing cycle (generally monthly), the lawyer (or the billing partner) will review the gross billable hours logged in the prior month and make adjustments to reflect inefficiencies, misstatements, etc. It is not unusual for this adjustments to be in the 5 to 10 percent range. Assume in the above example, that WIP write-offs are 7.5 percent. The "worth" of the prior $25,000 has now declined to $23,125.

After the bill is submitted to the client, she will often review it for accuracy and dispute some changes. Frequently law firms will make accommodations for their better clients and write off additional amounts. Assume in the case of our hypothetical client that these adjustments count for another 5 percent. The net account receivable has now been reduced to $21,875.

All this back and forth negotiation takes time. In recessionary periods, clients are hardly clamoring to pay their lawyer's bills within thirty days. It is not unusual for even the best-run law firms to have more than 30 percent of their accounts receivable be outstanding more than ninety days.

Although few lawyers appear to understand the elementary concept of the time value of money, it is a theory based in everyday logic. By permitting clients to postpone payment on large accounts receivable, law firms are acting as a bank. Any commercial enterprise that permits its customers to take merchandise off the shelf and use it for six months without paying for it will be in deep doo-doo in short order. It would be in even more trouble if it *rewarded* its sales staff on the basis of permitting customers to take merchandise, *reducing* the price after the "sale," and still not being paid. That is exactly what firms that cleave to the gross billable hours standard do.

In the example above, when the client finally pays the bill (reduced by 1 percent a month for purposes of this illustration), the net receipts to the firm is effectively $21,121—substantially less than the amount originally contemplated.

When partners are paid on the basis of gross hours rather than the net funds actually realized, it creates horrendous distortions in calculations of "worth."

It is not difficult to correct these problems. A firm should make it a policy not to make *any* compensation decisions based upon gross billable hours but rather upon net amounts received.

These net amounts can be clearly tracked to partners' work, reduced by the WIP write-offs, accounts receivable write-offs, and the time value of money "loaned" to clients.

Partners simply must be given incentive to collect outstanding fees promptly. The best way to accomplish this is to make sure that delays in payments are reflected in partners' compensation.

CHAPTER 17

Partner Compensation: The Cost Side

Some firm overhead costs should be mutually shared. These include rent, utilities, and business office staff. In most law firms, however, there are partners who use considerably more resources than others. Some partners, for example, use enormous numbers of associates and legal assistants for preparing law review articles, demand palatial offices, and even two or three secretaries.

While these expenses may be justified by the ego of the partner concerned, they may not be related to that lawyer's overall productivity in terms of net income.

Partners in law firms, like mere mortals, need daily reminders of the amount of money they are wasting and to be motivated to either spend the money to satisfy their visions of office grandeur or save it so they can buy summer palazzos in the Catskills.

The best way to do this is by bifurcating the compensation system into at least two pools—a "cost pool" and an "income pool." The cost pool should be subdivided in to mutually shared costs and individual costs. The percentages allocated to each of the subpools in the cost pool is a decision each firm should make. Nevertheless, it should be clear that excessive use of firm resources by an individual partner should at least be partially borne by that partner.

If Throgmorton Parsimony III is perfectly satisfied with monklike accommodations and sharing a secretary with three associates, should he be expected to pay the same overhead as Jimmy Goodvibes down the hall who demands a bowling-alley-sized office, two secretaries, and a platoon of legal assistants to do research for his latest article in the *Journal of American Ambulance Catchers?*

"Baselines" for what the firm will cover should be established, and anything over these baselines should be billed directly to the partner. If a partner wants a palatial office, a bevy of legal assistants, or pre-Khomeini Persian carpets on his floor, that's fine—so long as he pays for them.

The inequitable consumption of the resources of the firm is as much a cause for dissension as is the inequitable distribution of income. Few lawyers would begrudge a partner a coliseum-sized office with a trophy room if it was clearly understood that the expense of that excess was paid for directly by the Nero concerned.

It is important that a firm adopt a written policy concerning this and incorporate it in the partnership agreement. Unlike the subjective questions that inevitably arise with regard to "credits" given for client development, excessive overhead costs can be objectively computed.

A partner can know in advance that if he assigns an associate to do a research project for his latest book, he will be responsible for paying a portion of the associate's unbillable hours.

As noted above, the firm should establish baselines for partners' overhead. This can be done either as a percentage of all overhead (e.g., each partner is allocated 50 percent of total overhead with the balance being paid for by the individual partner, depending upon use) or on the basis of "line items." In either case, a system must be developed to track partners' actual use of firm resources. The following are some of the major areas that should be considered in developing a firm baseline system.

♦ Personnel costs. The single largest partner use of firm resources is generally personnel. A free-market-oriented law firm does not want to discourage the use of firm personnel; it merely wants to assure that these resources are used efficiently.

Assume, for example, that Partner A and Partner B both use 1,000 hours of associates' time in a given year. Suppose Partner A *collects* fees from clients of $130,000. Partner B's clients pay only $80,000. A free-market law firm would charge both partners the same amount on the cost side of the ledger for the use of firm resources. Partner A, however, will more than cover his costs on the income side of the ledger. This system encourages a leveraging, but most of all, it motivates partners to be judicious in the assignments they give to associates and rewards partners most for using firm resources efficiently.

Partners will protest that it is essential to their practice that they use legal assistants to prepare law review articles, etc., on the grounds that such articles help them in their business promotion. This may be true and, if it is, should show up (eventually) on the income side. If it is not true, however, the partner using firm resources for these purposes should still be required to pay for them.

Sometimes personnel are required to perform services for the firm in general (service on firm committees, Bar Association functions, etc.). These services can be built into the firm's baseline of overhead and not allocated to individual partners.

The firm can also have a policy of "special circumstances" in which individual staff members' overhead is blended into the general firm overhead. This should be a matter of written policy and not within the sole discretion of an individual partner.

♦ Secretarial time. Secretaries should generally be regarded as general firm overhead. There are instances, however, where partners should be expected to pay additional for secretarial services. In some firms, senior partners often believe that their volume of work warrants having two, and even three, secretaries to cater to their whims. This need not be a topic of serious debate in a law firm.

If His Excellency, the "named" senior partner, needs three secretaries—fine—so long as he personally pays for the costs above his baseline allocation. If he is really as good as he thinks he is, he'll more than cover his costs by the increased income he derives therefrom. The firm, however, should not be expected to pay for setting up tee times for his majesty.

♦ Other Firm Overhead. Although use of firm personnel almost always represents the largest cost discrepancy among partners, there are areas where partners consume disproportionate amounts of firm costs. These include: larger than standard offices, use of firm cars, and use of firm facilities for personal purposes.

It should be noted that partners, like all firm employees, should be expected to pay 100 percent when they put firm facilities to personal use (postage for personal mailing, personal photocopying, personal long-distance telephone calls, etc.).

Some partners, however, also use firm facilities for matters which are not strictly personal (service on Bar Association matters is one example). While these matters may be good for the firm eventually, they can be expensive in the short run, and partners should be expected to pay a portion of them.

"The law is a sort of hocus-pocus science that smiles in your face while it picks your pocket."

H.L. Mencken

CHAPTER 18

Partner Compensation: The Income Side

Partners in law firms argue endlessly over the appropriate method for compensating themselves and their brethren. In former times, many firms operated on a strict seniority basis, with the most senior partners automatically receiving the highest compensation. Raises were in lockstep. The inequities of a system such as this are apparent. It effectively penalizes bright young partners who collect extraordinary fees and secure new business while rewarding ossified old codgers whose careers are on the wane.

Other firms adopted an "eat what you kill" approach, dividing the partnership pie along the lines of who brought the business to the firm. This rewards rainmakers at the expense of people who were less skilled in client acquisition but are first-class lawyers. Another problem with the "eat what you kill" approach, particularly for mature firms, is that many clients tended to become institutional, and in some firms, the billing partner for a particular client was not even born when the client was acquired.

Partners are fond of pointing out that since the billing partner had no role in acquiring the client in the first place being compensated for being the billing partner under these circumstances is absurd.

Still other firms adopted a semifeudal system in which an individual or small "compensation committee" met secretly and after interminable sessions of tarot-card readings and the throwing of chicken bones, came up with a list of compensation rates which were announced to the partnership, often with minimal rights of appeal.

Given all of the problems with other forms for determining compensation, firms in the midseventies increasingly relied on the gross billable standard for determining compensation. In most law firms, it is the primary, if not the only measure of an attorney's contribution to the firm.

Nevertheless, the gross billable hours standard, while it may measure physical presence in an office, is no more reflective of the value of a partner's contribution to the law firm than any of the other tried and discarded mechanisms. While it is true that all the factors addressed by these systems should go into determining partner compensation (client acquisition, work product, diligence, loyalty, management, etc.) the most fundamental flaw of the gross billable hours standard is not that it just ignores the other essential ingredients to a successful law firm, but it is based upon a mirage.

Gross billable hours do not necessarily represent income. As previously noted, gross billable hours are often written off, written down, or languish for months without being paid.

In determining partnership compensation, it is essential to focus on *income* rather than mere numbers on a time sheet. This is the cardinal rule of establishing a rational basis for compensation of partners.

Any partner compensation system should be as objective as possible but retain a degree of discretion "at the margins" to allow for such factors a management responsibilities, extraordinary effort, and anomalies in collections. Nevertheless, for a law firm to prosper in a free-market economy, there should be understandable objective standards by which partners are compensated. These should be enumerated clearly in a written policy and incorporated into the partnership agreement.

With these two principles in mind, a rational partner compensation system can be devised that incorporates all of the factors which make law firms prosper, while allowing greater flexibility among partners to peruse their individual interests and strengths. To be successful, compensation policy must satisfy four criteria:

◆ Will it satisfy the billing partner under most circumstances?

◆ Will it motivate the rainmaker to continue to bring in business under most circumstances?

◆ Does it fairly compensate other partners who have anything to do with the matter?

◆ Will it encourage crossmarketing (will all the partners receive their own economic interest, or are they well served in moving business to other partners)?

The best-designed compensation schemes allow a partner to choose his own compensation and incorporates the cost elements with income. This generally requires the establishment of two pools. The cost pool, the elements of which have been reviewed previously, and the "income pool."

The income pool in a free-market law firm takes into consideration each of the elements noted above in separate subpools. The percentages of income in each subpool are a matter for each firm to determine based upon its culture. Nevertheless, every free-market law firm should consider the following procedure:

NET INCOME

Partner Work Product

Synopsis: A portion of the total net income pool should be earmarked to "partner work product." This percentage, like all others in this process, is discretionary. Firm management can determine the relative size of the pools. This pool is designed to encourage partners to maximize their *net* collections. Partners are rewarded for working for clients who pay their bills timeously and can increase their *personal* income by working an appropriate number of hours. Compensation in this subpool also reflects the partner's billing rate.

The Partner Work Product pool can be modified to suit the preferences of the firm. For example, some firms may wish to include only the actual amounts billed by the partners, others may choose to include amounts billed by other attorneys and legal assistants the partner has supervised. It should be noted, however, that this subpool, like all others in the income pool, is based upon actual income received—not work on work in process or accounts receivable.

A partner shares in this pool to the extent that the work accomplished is actually paid for by the client(s). It encourages partners to work the most on matters with the greatest chance of recovery. Risk taking is, therefore, primarily at the discretion of the partner. If a partner believes there is a good chance that the client will pay, he performs the work. If the client is a likely deadbeat, the partner would think twice about undertaking vast amounts of gross billable hours. This substantially reduces the chance that there will be significant work in process or accounts receivable write-offs, since the partner will be reluctant to undertake marginal cases in the first place.

This pool is intended to reward partners for their work on any firm client (whether the partner "originated" the client or not) and is designed to encourage sharing of client work.

Client Acquisition

Synopsis: Client acquisition is one of the most important factors affecting firm growth. A compensation plan should reward partners who are successful in attracting new clients to the firm *regardless* of how many gross billable hours that partner logs. At the same time, it should be recognized that after a period, a client should be regarded as a firm or institutional client and that a partner cannot benefit *forever* by merely bringing in a large matter in a given year. These goals can be accomplished by a system that rewards new client (or matter) acquisition immediately but phases out such rewards over time.

It is important to recognize that "business development" activities, while critical to client acquisition, should *not* be rewarded absent a clear demonstration of their success. The *only* reasonable measurement of business development plans is *net receipts* from new clients or matters. Note that under the system described here, a partner would pay for a portion of his or her client development expenses. If these projects are successful, they will be rewarded in this pool.

The value for this pool is determined by reviewing the *net* receipts for the month in question and determining which of those receipts qualify as new business or a new matter. As noted above, some clients or matters should be regarded as institutional and are *not* eligible for inclusion in the pool.

Generally, a client or matter will be regarded as institutional after a set number of years, ranging from two to ten. Further, "credit" for acquiring a new client or matter should *decline* during that period. "Points" are awarded for acquiring new clients/matters. A freshly minted client will be awarded the maximum number of points the first year, but these points decline annually until the client is regarded as institutional. A rainmaker partner will be rewarded for her ongoing efforts to replenish the client base whether she actually works on those client's matter or not.

This system also rewards not just client acquisition but acquiring *profitable* clients.

It should be noted that "new matters" for an "old" client *may* be given points *even though* the client is an institutional client. *Only* receipts from that new matter, however, are eligible for receiving such points.

The determination of which partners are responsible for new client/new matter acquisition is somewhat subjective but can generally be resolved on a negotiated basis.

New clients (or matters) come to the firm under literally hundreds of circumstances. The examples below are meant to illustrate only some of the methods by which credit can be apportioned to the relevant partners:

Client A was brought to the firm solely through the efforts of Partner A (the president of the company is his sister-in-law). Here, Partner A receives the entire value of the points.

Client B was retained by the firm as a result of a joint effort between Partners B and C. They split the points 50/50. Each receives half of the points available.

Client C was retained by the firm largely through the efforts of Partner D, whose "marketing plan" emphasized the expertise of Partner E. Assume E did nothing, but her expertise was the *reason* the client retained the firm. Through negotiations, the partners agree Partner D receives 66.66 percent of the points and Partner E 33.33 percent.

Seniority

Synopsis: The seniority pool rewards service to the firm and implicitly acknowledges experience. Points are awarded at a rate of one per year for service with the firm (either as a partner or an attorney) up to a set maximum number designed by firm management. As with other pools, the percentage of firm income in the seniority pool can also be adjusted to accommodate individual firm requirements.

Total net income for this pool is divided by the total number of points available for the entire partnership. Each point is assigned a dollar value multiplied by the total number of points held by that particular partner. For example, assume $5 million in net income in a particular month.

Step 1. Determine the dollar amount to be allocated to this pool.

$5 million total net income x 15% (the percentage allocated to seniority pool by that firm) = $750,000.

Step 2. Determine the number of points available. Points are awarded on the basis of one point for each year of service either as a partner or with the firm (this to be determined by the firm).

Step 3. Determine point value.

Assume: That the total number of points is 1,500 (*i.e.*, total seniority points for *all* partners).

$750,000/1,500 (total points) = $50/point

Step 3. Determine compensation for partner from this pool.

Assume: Partner A has 17 points (17 years seniority):
17 x $50 = $850

Discretionary Pool

The "discretionary" pool is designed to permit the firm management to reward partners for extraordinary effort on behalf of the firm, regardless of any other consideration. This pool would be particularly useful in compensating partners for administrative or committee work which would detract from their ability to log hours. It would also be used to recognize partners who performed extensive pro bono services or who contribute significantly to the growth of the firm.

CHAPTER 19

Chucking Deadwood

Some law firms unceremoniously dump partners when they have reached the limits of their productivity. This is not a good idea. Senior partners can bring prestige, expertise, and significant experience to any law firm and often are an attraction to clients. The problem is not getting rid of "deadwood" but overcompensating unproductive partners. If a firm adopts an objective basis for compensation, which includes both charging partners for the costs that they incur and rewarding them for the work they do and the business they bring in, the problem takes care of itself. So-called "deadwood" can be an asset to a firm, but the firm need not overpay for the services of senior counsel.

A clearly established compensation formula rewarding people for their contributions to the firm in terms of net income and charging partners for their costs to the firm can allow senior attorneys to make choices. Either they stay in their prestigious position at lower compensation, or they retire. The lower compensation rates should be known in advance as a matter of firm policy and not be subjective. Kicking out the old geezers (particularly if they are name partners) rarely enhances the reputation of the firm among clients. A firm that allows a graceful winding down in terms of compensation, permits the individual involved to achieve emeritus status without burdening the firm with excessive compensation requirements.

In one major law firm, a very senior partner has a magnificent office, works hours a banker would admire, has access to the firm limousine, attends partners meetings regularly—and receives no compensation at all. His costs are covered by the income from his clients. His ego is satisfied. His wife is happy because he's not grousing at home, and the clients still revere him. This is a sensitive, businesslike alternative to booting the old goat out the door.

CHAPTER 20

Learn to Compete I: Pricing Your Product

One of the most difficult aspects of the transition from a gross billable hours culture to a free-market system is to reverse a firm culture that emphasizes inefficiency. Free-market firms put a premium on keeping hours as low as possible, while gross billable hours firms encourage people to work as long as possible. This culture shock can be daunting, but there are ways to make the transition easier.

The most essential aspect of the transition to a free-market system is to have a written policy committing the organization to this goal. The second is to directly link partners' compensation to the realization of those goals by motivating partners to cut costs, collect receivables, and work efficiently. Once those policies are in place, the firm is in a position to adopt a series of measures to enhance its profitability.

One of the most important factors in establishing efficiency is to set targets for pricing your product. Traditionally, law firms have paid little attention to this. They didn't need to. A product was billed at whatever time it took to make it. In gross billable hours firms, it was often more profitable to adopt a "Blue Sky" approach to every will, initial public offering, or divorce settlement. Each document was written from scratch as if it were the first one ever produced. This took a substantially greater number of hours than utilizing other available resources.

Despite what many lawyers think, it is possible to establish targets for pricing almost any legal matter. These targets are not exact, but sophisticated firms can generally hit their targets plus or minus 10 percent with a bit of practice. Establishing targets puts a premium on efficiency in that the fewer hours necessary to achieve a particular objective, the more profitable each of those hours is.

Establishing target rates is sometimes a tedious task. Nevertheless, it is essential to the transition of a firm to a free market.

Consider just the first step—establishing the *principle* of target pricing. The following are merely examples of how this might be done.

1. Establish a manual listing target bills for various legal matters. Some firms have found it useful to review projects on which they have worked in the past year to get an idea of how well (or poorly) they performed certain legal functions. For example, assume that a mid-sized firm prepared five wills in the prior cal-

endar year. Reference to time sheets and billing memoranda reveal the following:

Will #1:

5 hours at @$250/hr.	=	$1,250
15 hours at $150/hr	=	2,250
		$3,500

Will #2:

7 hours @ $250/hr.	=	$1,750
5 hours @ $175/hr.	=	875
		$2,625

Will #3:

2 hours @ $250/hr.	=	$ 500
20 hours @ $125/hr.	=	2,500
		$3,000

Will #4:

10 hours @ $250/hr.	=	$2,500
5 hours @ $175/hr.	=	875
		$3,375

Will #5:

15 hours @ $250/hr.	=	$3,750
22 hours @ $175/hr.	=	3,850
10 hours @ $150/hr.	=	1,500
		$9,100

The preparation of these wills varied greatly both in time and cost. After representative wills have been identified, an independent committee should examine the final products. This committee should *not* include anyone responsible for the initial work. They will be consulted but should not be part of the analysis at this stage.

The committee should place the wills side by side to determine their equivalency. Wills, like fingerprints, are generally unique but will have certain common characteristics. The wills should be examined by the committee to determine the extent to which they are similar and dissimilar. Unique legal questions can add time and expense to preparation of any legal document, but experienced counsel should be able to prepare a document in a minimum of time whereas counsel unfamiliar with the topic will take longer. Matrixes should be made for each of the documents as follows, with complexity rated on a scale of 1 to 10 and uniqueness on the same scale where 1 is plain vanilla and 10 is truly bizarre:

Will #1:

Pages___7___

Complexity___5___

Uniqueness___4___

Will #2:

Pages___7___

Complexity___5___

Uniqueness___3___

Will #3:

Pages___9___

Complexity___4___

Uniqueness___5___

Will #4:

Pages___10___

Complexity___3___

Uniqueness___3___

Will #5:

Pages___13___

Complexity___8___

Uniqueness___7___

As can be seen from this analysis, the complexity and uniqueness of a particular will is not necessarily reflected in its price. The authors of Will #2, for example, produced a product in a minimum amount of time. Particularly when contrasted with Will #4 (a will of lesser complexity and uniqueness), the client received a much higher value. Perhaps this was because of experience or better utilization of resources.

In a firm grounded in gross billable hours, the authors of Will #5 would have been the *least* productive for the client. Although this will was more complex than the others, the cost was almost four times the price of Will #2 but only twice as difficult.

The above exercise is only the first step in developing price schedules for legal work. Before adequate schedules can be written, the firm must be able to identify existing problems as well as examples of where individuals in the firm have been able to produce services at reasonable cost.

After this first step has been taken, the individuals responsible for each of the wills should be interviewed to determine the reasons for the discrepancies. Sometimes these will be obvious. For example, a particular client may have insisted upon numerous meetings with the lawyers involved, which ran up costs; another client may have come with written instructions to the drafters, which substantially reduced their time.

Even after all of these explanations, it will be obvious that some legal work was done much more efficiently than others. It would be unusual for a firm to go through an exercise as above and not be able to identify areas where there are wide variations in both time and charges for equivalent work. The objective of a free-market law firm is to recognize areas where it already is acting efficiently and try to move everyone closer to that standard while improving the standard itself.

The above example is crude. The next chapter discusses computer modeling which enables law firms to accurately track time, charges, and expenses.

Although gross billable hours firms tend to discourage fixed billing, this sometimes occurs and provides another opportunity for measuring efficiency. Fixed fee billing in gross billable hours firms can lead to a number of anomalies (e.g., attorney's "loading" time sheets, thus disguising potential efficiencies). Even these sometimes are not enough to camouflage the profitability that can result from increased efficiency.

The standard of the net realized hourly rate is one of the best indicators of efficiency. This standard can be illustrated as follows. A law firm undertakes two similar projects—one on a fixed fee basis and the other on a gross billable hour basis.

Issue A (gross billable hours basis).

6 hours @ $225/hr.	=	$1,350
10 hours @ $150/hr.	=	1,500
15 hours @ $ 75/hr.	=	1,125
TOTAL		$3,975

Issue B (fixed fee basis—assuming a fixed fee of $3,500].

Attorney A—3 hrs. [nominal rate = $225/hr.] = $ 675
Attorney B—7 hrs. [nominal rate = $150/hr.] = 1,050
Paralegal C—10 hrs. [nominal rate = $75/hr.] = 750

Fees if computed on gross billable hrs. basis: $2,475
Actual fees: $3,500

Net realized hourly rates for Issue B:

Attorney A—$318/hr.
Attorney B—$212/hr.
Paralegal C—$106/hr.

As can be seen from the above example, even though the fixed fee was *lower* than the fee generated by gross billable hours, the net hourly rate for the attorneys involved in Issue B was 40 percent *higher* than for Issue A. In this example, the client benefits from a lower rate; the firm is rewarded by its greater efficiency.

CHAPTER 21

Matter Management

For years, corporate law departments of major companies have used computerized "matter management" systems to track the relative efficiency of outside law firms. To date, however, few freestanding law firms have the slightest idea of what these systems can do. In fact, they are as useful in analyzing a firm's own efficiency as they are for in-house counsel to track the relative costs of vendors. Further, they can be an invaluable resource for analyzing and predicting costs of almost any legal service and have a relatively untapped potential for enabling law firms to prepare competitive bids for legal projects.

While there are dozens of computerized matter management systems, almost all of them perform at least the following functions:

Matter Tracking. Captures detailed information about matters, including identifying characteristics, status, and major issues.

These systems provide quick access to information through on-line queries and reports.

Fee or Invoice Tracking. Tracks fees and other expenses charged. Some matter management systems also include a module for allocating legal costs to business units.

Accounts Payable/Receivable. Some matter management systems provide accounts payable/receivable modules that receive data directly from the fee-tracking module. This allows the client (or the law firm) to monitor outstanding bills and payments. In other cases, there may be an interface to a third-party accounts payable system.

Timekeeping. Tracks the time each attorney charges to a particular matter.

Budgeting. Allows the client (or the law firm) to establish budgets for each legal matter and to determine whether budgetary targets are being met on a day-to-day basis.

File Management. Tracks the location and disposal of files related to a particular client matter.

Docket and Calendar. Records important events as a client matter progresses and includes some form of "tickler" to notify staff of impending deadlines.

As originally conceived, matter management systems were designed to assist lawyers in litigation but have become so sophisticated that they can track costs associated with each matter against a negotiated norm.

Many inside counsel use matter management systems to select law firms, comparing various outside counsel's performance against standards that are built into the systems. Almost incredibly, however, most law firms have not used existing software to track their own performance.

This management tool is readily available, and since customers are already using them defensively, it is astonishing more law firms have not adopted these as a matter of self-defense. These systems are now so sophisticated that companies such as Wal-Mart, Bank One, Michigan National Bank, and Chrysler can simultaneously compare the performance of various firms against each other for similar matters.

The systems can compare various departments within a law firm for relative productivity on a net realized basis, even down to the level of individual paralegal assistants. It can be a daunting experience to have the general counsel of a major company tell you that your primary competition handles matters more efficiently than that you do and has the figures to prove it.

It is not the purpose of this book to analyze the various software programs available. Other publications do a good job of that, including those of the section on legal economics of the American Bar Association and the Corporate Counsel Association. It should be noted that there are so many software programs available that a system can be found that is adaptable to almost any hardware currently used by law firms. There are mainframe, as well as PC and LAN versions, which are used in companies around the country.

Only a tiny portion of these systems, however, are currently in use in law firms (except in litigation management). Their adaptability, however, is clear.

This is an area where inside counsel has can offer valuable experience to their outside vendors. One major law firm even recently "raided" one of its own clients of its computer guru to help establish its own system. This is a resource that cannot be overlooked and should be immediately adopted by any law firm intending to be a serious player in a free-market economy.

CHAPTER 22

Marketing

Some gross billable hours firms have recognized that in the competitive nineties, marketing is essential. The competition is simply too intense to rely on clients who (a) realize they need legal services and (b) choose you.

It is an exercise in folly, however, for a gross billable hours-oriented firm merely to hire a "marketing director" and expect that problems will be solved. The basic ethic of the firm must be addressed first.

If partners are not rewarded for their relative success in acquiring clients and do not see their income or advancement in the firm enhanced by marketing efforts, they are unlikely to support a marketing department. In fact, some aggressive partners who exist in firms that adopt the gross billable hours philosophy will regard the marketing department as a threat in that their success in acquiring clients will be attributed to someone else.

Still, it is a truism that lawyers are to marketing what devout Muslims are to barbecued spareribs—they simply know nothing about it.

A "marketing coordinator," as opposed to a "marketing director," is appropriate for many firms that have adopted the free-market philosophy. The job description for a marketing coordinator can include many duties:

◆ Preparing standardized resumes (short and long form) for all attorneys in the firm.

◆ Preparing practice descriptions for each of the firm's areas of expertise.

◆ Arranging and coordinating publicity efforts for particular successes that the firm has had and dealing with the press in general.

◆ Arranging for attorneys' participation in seminars and other public forums.

◆ Identifying new client prospects and providing a synopsis of these potential new clients to relevant attorneys.

◆ Arranging for firm receptions for clients and assisting attorneys in "beauty shows" in a competitive environment.

◆ Preparing standardized firm presentation materials, including brochures, covers, and other promotional materials.

◆ Developing and maintaining client relations calendars which remind attorneys to contact clients, potential clients, and former clients on particularly significant dates.

In short, a marketing director should act more as a coordinator of general firm marketing efforts than taking the place of marketing efforts of the firm. This is essentially an administrative position to see to it that the firm's marketing policies are implemented. It will require the commitments of the entire firm, however, for any marketing scheme to be successful.

While it is not the purpose of this book to describe in detail the technicalities of the different marketing methods a firm can employ to sell its services, before a firm can be successful in any marketing activities, it must accept the realities of the free market.

Oddly, this is one of the most difficult tasks for many traditional firms which regard marketing as distasteful, at best, and unprofessional, at worst. The truth is that marketing is essential in today's competitive legal markets. A free-market-oriented firm should approach the problem from a slightly different perspective than others.

Since many firms offer similar legal services, are comparably equipped with computers, and have access to research material through on-line data systems, free-market firms should emphasize their strengths. They can translate the efficiency and expertise they have into savings for their clients—both in time and in money. Some free-market firms even acknowledge that they, and their competitors, can deliver a similar quality legal product but emphasize that their product gets there faster—and at substantially less cost than their rivals.

Promotional materials of free-market firms accentuate this difference. One free-market firm brochure illustrates two apparently identical legal briefs, one with a price tag of $12,000 -delivery time six weeks—the other with a price tag of $5,000—delivery time two weeks. The caption says these two products are virtually identical, but which would you rather have? Although hardly innovative in the world of advertising, an approach emphasizing value and timeliness is almost an alien concept in the legal community. Firms that attempted this have been astonished by its success with their clients.

Once a marketing philosophy is adopted that focuses on the strengths that the free-market philosophy gives a firm, the opportunities for selling this concept are almost endless. A firm need not embrace tacky late-night television ads employed by some ambulance-chasing personal injury lawyers to develop a highly effective campaign.

One of the most important documents that a firm can employ in this regard is a (short) statement of principles, explaining how its work is done, how its fees are structured, and how its attorneys are compensated. Some attorneys are horrified by this prospect, but it is important. Other types of retail establishments emphasize this point noting that salespersons are paid salaries, not commissions. An assurance to clients that attorneys are not paid on the basis of the *most* time it takes them can be a remarkably successful marketing tool.

There are other ways to draw this fact to the attention of clients. Dozens of articles have been written on this subject, and even one book—the one you're holding. A client might want to know that your firm has adopted free-market principles and an outline of how you have done so. (*Author's Note*: The preceding two sentences are examples of the type of shameless hype that a law firm might want to consider.)

Some lawyers will object that total reliance on fixed fees carries with it as many problems as does total reliance on gross billable hours for billing and compensation. There are, indeed, many areas where fixed fees can lead to anomalous results. Further, total reliance on fixed fees may encounter significant opposition from certain clients. As noted in Book I, however, a free-market law firm need not adopt a total fixed fee approach—fees can be negotiated to take account of changed circumstances.

Imagine negotiating a contract for remodeling your home. Few people would sign a "time and materials" contract in that the total price is open ended. Most homeowners would prefer a fixed price and require the contractor to perform more efficiently.

Even here, however, there can be changes. These can include alterations to the original plan. You may decide you want the light switches on the south wall rather than the west wall. Unexpected difficulties can pop up—it rained the entire week they were supposed to put your new roof on—and as can legal problems—your neighbors object to your painting your house fuchsia, and you have to go to court to defend your decision.

Agreements with clients for the performance of legal services should also have sufficient flexibility so neither the attorney nor the client is ambushed by unexpected windfalls or problems. This may, in certain circumstances, involve blended rates; in others, an agreement with regard to fixed prices for extra services not covered by the primary agreement.

Notwithstanding these problems, it should be clear to both the client and the law firm that neither party will be "burned" by the agreement and that the firm will be motivated to work as efficiently as possible to achieve the desired results.

"Apologists for the profession contend that lawyers are as honest as other men, but this is not very encouraging."

Ferdinand Lundberg, author of
The Natural Depravity of Mankind

Epilogue

Despite the image of lawyers being reptiles (an image they have largely brought upon themselves), most attorneys are honorable and try to do their very best for their clients. By removing the incentives to "bump" bills, however, both clients *and* law firms can return the profession of law to the esteem in which it was once held.

I hope that this book is not regarded as yet another "lawyer-bashing" tome but rather a wake-up call to lawyers and lay alike to return professionalism to the legal profession while recognizing the essential business aspects of the practice of law.